BEAN CUISINE

METRO BOOKS
New York

An Imprint of Sterling Publishing
387 Park Avenue South
New York, NY 10016

Conceived, edited, and designed by
Marshall Editions
The Old Brewery, 6 Blundell Street
London N7 9BH
www.marshalleditions.com

Editorial Director Sorrel Wood
Copy Editor Donna Gregory
Editorial Assistant Philippa Davis
Proofreader Jane Bamforth
Design Lucy Parissi
Photography Simon Pask
Food Styling Genevieve Taylor
Production Nikki Ingram

ISBN 978-1-4351-5123-9

*For information about custom editions, special sales, and premium and corporate purchases,
please contact Sterling Special Sales at 800-805-5489 or specialsales@sterlingpublishing.com.*

Printed in China

2 4 6 8 10 9 7 5 3 1

www.sterlingpublishing.com

BEAN CUISINE

100 naturally delicious recipes that are low-fat and super nutritious

GENEVIEVE TAYLOR

METRO BOOKS
New York

CONTENTS

INTRODUCTION

BEANS, BEANS, BEANS

EASY EVERYDAY BEANS

52

BEAN FEASTS

2

76

BEANS TO GO

3

82

SNACKS AND DIPS

4

114

SWEET BEANS

5

128

FOR THE LOVE OF BEANS

I love, love, love beans! This humble ingredient is genuinely one of my very favorite things to experiment with in the kitchen. Beans and pulses are inexpensive, filling, and nutritious—I guess we all knew that—but I hope to show you that beans can also be exciting, elegant, refined, indulgent, exotic—even sweet. No longer the sole preserve of wholefood devotees, bean cookery has truly come a long way in recent years. Once a relatively infrequently used pantry staple in my own kitchen, I can proudly say that beans are now center stage in my cooking. Whether you use canned beans, or with a little more planning, dried beans, the recipes in this book are great for feeding your family.

For me, one of the best things about beans is how brilliant they are at absorbing the flavors of a host of herbs and spices. Cuisines from all over the world—Mexican, Moroccan, Indian, Japanese, and Mediterranean to name but a few—all use them to great effect. Most beans have a relatively mild flavor and this allows for ultimate versatility and flexibility in cooking, as they pretty much go with everything.

One of the more surprising areas in which beans can excel is their use in sweet dishes. They are wonderful in traditional Asian puddings, such as the red bean soup or the mooncake cookies on page 134 and page 122, but they also turn up in all-American favorites. The cannellini bean, white chocolate, and hazelnut blondies on page 136 are guaranteed to be the moistest you have ever eaten, with the added bonus of more fiber and nutrients than a standard blondie. I have found baking with beans to be one of the easiest ways to get a little extra wholesomeness into my kids' diets. And by adding a few beans to your fruity breakfast smoothie you are adding a valuable boost of goodness that will fuel your whole morning (see page 126).

While not being the exclusive preserve of vegetarians, and there are plenty of delicious recipes here that include meat, we can all benefit from getting a little more of our protein from plant-based sources. In addition, by cooking more with beans in place of meat, you can be assured you are reducing your carbon footprint significantly. Personally, I try to eat beans at least three times a week, sometimes using a meat as a flavoring—it's amazing how much intensity a little chorizo or pancetta can bring to a bean-based dish. You will also find the recipes in the book invaluable for when vegetarian or vegan friends come to visit.

Most of all, I hope to show you how easy it is to elevate beans from the wholesome to the elegant. With a bit of love they can be turned into something surprisingly rich and even decadent while still retaining their goodness. Beans really have it all going for them.

HOW TO USE THIS BOOK

The recipes in this book suit all tastes and diets. Each carefully thought-out recipe will deliver new flavors, fresh cooking methods, and delicious new ingredients.

At the front of the book you can find all the information you need about different kinds of beans, how they are sold, and how to cook them to get the best results

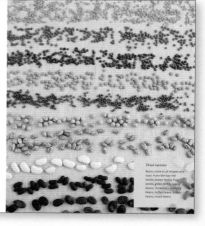

Before you start, find out how many people each recipe serves, plus how long you need for preparation and cooking

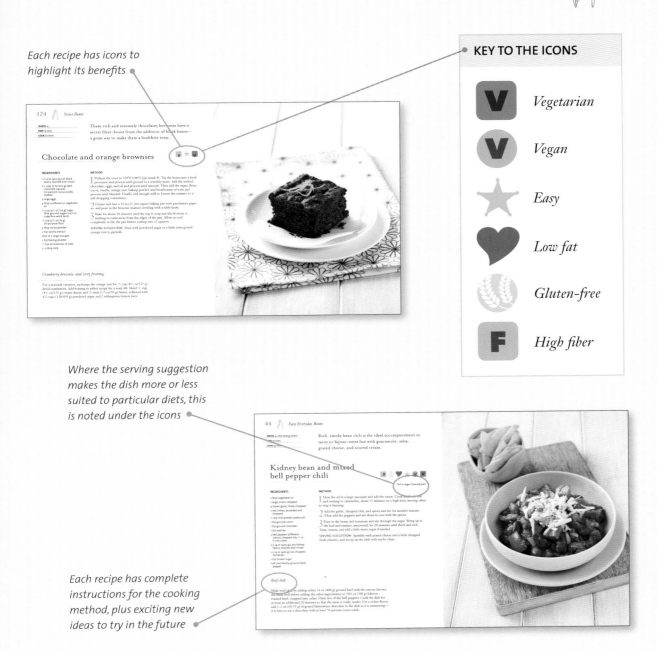

Each recipe has icons to highlight its benefits

KEY TO THE ICONS

V *Vegetarian*

V *Vegan*

★ *Easy*

♥ *Low fat*

Gluten-free

F *High fiber*

Where the serving suggestion makes the dish more or less suited to particular diets, this is noted under the icons

Each recipe has complete instructions for the cooking method, plus exciting new ideas to try in the future

At the back of the book there is a useful index so you can look up recipes by type of bean

BEANS, BEANS, BEANS

Easy and quick to prepare, there are lots of delicious varieties of beans and pulses to try. Most recipes in this book use canned or fresh beans, but you can make the recipes even more cost-effective by cooking the beans from dried yourself.

THE BENEFITS OF BEANS

As a food, beans have got it going on. They are healthy, versatile, and delicious. From a nutritional point of view, it would be tough to improve on the goodness contained within the humble bean.

The top 10 *beanefits*

1 Supremely economical, you will save a huge amount at the grocery store by cooking with beans several times a week.

2 Beans are 20–25% protein, twice that of wheat and three times that of rice.

3 Low glycemic index—so beans are great at stabilizing blood sugar levels after meals.

4 One cup of beans contains half the recommended daily adult fiber intake.

5 Cholesterol free and low in fat.

6 A good source of essential minerals, including iron, magnesium, phosphorus, and zinc.

7 High in folate and other B vitamins.

8 Gluten-free, so great for a celiac or wheat-free diet.

9 Low allergenicity, this means it is very rare for people to be allergic to beans.

10 Eating more beans instead of meat has widely recognized environmental benefits.

Beans are good news all around—high in fiber, low in fat, cholesterol free, and with high protein content, as well as being a good source of B vitamins and iron. Beans are also high in complex, slow-energy-releasing carbohydrates and have significant amounts of the important minerals copper, phosphorus, manganese, and magnesium. Beans are the original vegetarian superfood—benefiting diets long before tofu and faux-meat substitutes—and everyone nowadays could benefit from increasing the intake of beans in their diet.

Beans are not just good for you, they are also really easy to cook. With a bit of know-how and inspiration, a handful or two of cooked beans can be turned into an infinite variety of delicious meals.

Fresh and green beans

As explained in detail on page 16, fresh beans come in all shapes and sizes. Sometimes you eat the pod, sometimes just the beans themselves. Clockwise from top: runner beans, green beans, edamame, broad beans.

VARIETIES OF BEANS

Beans come in all colors, shapes, and sizes, and are often beautifully speckled and patterned. Despite their varied appearance, most of the beans we eat come from the different varieties bred from the common bean, *Phaseolus vulgaris*.

Genetically speaking, the varieties of beans we eat are all remarkably similar. This means that although each bean has slightly different characteristics, they are interchangeable in the kitchen. Peas, chickpeas, and lentils come from different plants we group together under the umbrella term, pulses. For the sake of avoiding repetition, these are all referred to, as a group, as beans in this book.

Dried lentils

Red lentils With a quick cooking time, these break down to a puree when tender, making them perfect for adding to soups and sauces. Popular in Indian and Middle Eastern cuisine, they are the essential ingredient in dal (see page 51).

Green lentils Small, medium, and large varieties are available. Popular in Mediterranean and Middle Eastern cuisine, these lentils retain their shape well when cooked.

Brown lentils Large, flat lentils with a solid skin that retain their shape during cooking, brown lentils have a slightly stronger flavor than green lentils (but one variety can easily be substituted for another).

Puy lentils Small, firm, slate gray lentils from Le Puy region in France, these are the only type of lentil to be identified by its area of cultivation. Much prized for their firm texture and slightly peppery flavor, they are great in salads (see page 80).

Dried peas (*Pisum sativum*)

These include whole dried peas and split peas. Split peas cook quickly without soaking, whole dried peas only need a short soak of an hour or so. Dried peas are excellent in soups, and are particularly popular in Middle Eastern cuisine.

Chickpeas (*garbanzo beans*) A large, round pulse with a strong nutty flavor, chickpeas are an essential ingredient in hummus and very popular in Middle Eastern and Indian cooking. They can also be ground to make chickpea (gram) flour, which is commonly used to make onion bhajis, or they can be roasted to make a healthy, nut-like snack (page 106).

Fresh beans

Green beans (*including string beans and French beans*) Quick to cook, various kinds of thin, round green beans are used widely throughout the world and there are more than 150 different varieties grown; a testament to their popularity. They are the unripe pods of specific varieties of the common bean (*Phaseolus vulgaris*).

Runner beans (*scarlet runner*) These long flat beans are not as commonly eaten as other green beans. In the United States, scarlet runners have been traditionally grown as ornamental plants, prized for their pretty, bright red flowers, but with a little careful cooking they are as delicious in the kitchen as they are beautiful in the garden. They can have tough strings down either side of the pod that are best trimmed off before cooking.

Soy beans Originally from eastern Asia, these beans are widely consumed the world over, usually in various processed forms such as soy milk, tofu, or textured vegetable protein. The immature beans can be eaten fresh and are commonly

known as edamame beans. Fresh soy beans are often sold frozen because, like fresh peas, they store very well in this form.

Broad beans *(fava beans)* Fresh broad beans are best eaten while still young and tender as they become tough with age. They are often sold frozen as baby broad beans. These beans really benefit from "double podding" before eating, especially if they are not very young. To do this, remove the beans from their outer green pods, and blanch the beans for 3–4 minutes. Run under cold water until they are cool enough to handle before squeezing each bean out of its tough outer shell. Broad beans are also available dried, and they are essential to Ful Medames, a delicious bean stew that is the Egyptian national dish. When dried, these beans need soaking and cooking in the same way as other dried beans (see page 22).

Canned beans

Flageolet beans Much prized in French cooking, flageolet beans are actually small, slightly underripe navy beans that have been harvested and dried before reaching full maturity. Small, oval, pale green, with a mild flavor, these beans cook beautifully to tender but will never take on the creamy texture of fully ripe navy beans.

Mung beans These small, firm, dark-green beans are hugely popular across Asia where they are often found in curries. They are also the bean used for producing beansprouts.

Butter beans *(lima bean)* Large flat white beans with a soft, creamy, slightly floury texture. Great in stews and for pureeing for dips, or mashing as a nutritious alternative to potatoes. Butter beans are perhaps the hardest bean to cook from dried. They have an irritating habit of going from rock hard to overly soft in a matter of minutes. For this reason butter beans are best bought canned and ready cooked.

Navy beans *(haricot beans, white pea beans)* Pea-sized beans that are creamy white in color. Mild flavored, dense, and smooth textured, these are traditionally used in baked beans (see page 52). Navy beans can be swapped for any other kind of white beans, such as cannellini or butter beans.

Cannellini beans *(great northern beans, large white beans)* These large, white, oval beans have a delicate flavor and soft texture. Very closely related to the navy bean, they can be easily interchanged in recipes.

Black-eyed peas *(cowpea)* Small, creamy-white beans with distinctive black eyes, these are commonly used in southern US cooking, but originally hail from Africa.

Cranberry beans *(borlotti beans)* A variety of kidney bean, with a white shell with deep cranberry pink striations, turning pinkish-brown on cooking. With a creamy texture, these beans are popular in Italian cooking, and can sometimes be found fresh in markets as well as dried or ready-

cooked in cans. It is also an easy bean to grow in the garden where their tall, twining stems are covered in lush, green, heart-shaped leaves.

Adzuki beans *(azuki, aduki bean)* These small, hard, red beans hail from Japan and China, and they are also used to make red bean paste, a sweet tasting paste used in many Asian cuisines and confectionery. Mung beans make a good substitute for adzuki beans.

Pinto beans Deep reddish brown stripes on light brown shells, turning a creamy, pinkish brown when cooked. Commonly used for refried beans and burritos. Cranberry beans make a good substitute for pinto beans.

Red kidney beans Vibrant color, strong flavor, named for its distinctive shape. Great in chilies, and their firm texture is great in salads or for adding to casseroles.

Black beans *(black turtle beans)* With deep black shells that hold their color when cooked, and creamy flesh inside, these beans are popular in Caribbean, South American, and Mexican cooking.

Canned beans

From the top, left to right: black beans, adzuki beans, flageolet beans, navy beans, black-eyed peas, cranberry beans.

A truly broad bean

Like most beans, broad beans can
be bought in all forms: canned,
fresh, frozen, or dried. Each recipe
recommends which kind to use.

TYPES OF BEANS FOR COOKING

Each recipe in this book recommends a particular type of bean to use—canned, fresh, dried, or frozen—but most of the recipes can be adapted to suit what you have to hand. Frozen and canned beans are the easiest to use because no preparation is required.

Dried, fresh, or canned?

For speed and convenience, there is no denying that canned, ready-cooked beans will win out every time. It's for this reason that most of the recipes in this book assume a starting point of canned beans. For simplicity and to avoid waste, most recipes use either one or two cans of ready-cooked beans. If you keep a few cans of ready-cooked beans in a kitchen cupboard you will always be ready to make something quick and nutritious. When using canned beans, be sure to drain them well and rinse under cold running water before adding the beans to your recipe.

However, if you have the time, then cooking beans from dried is more economical—a satisfyingly easy way to turn a cheap meal into a super frugal one. There is also the issue of reducing packaging waste. Although cans are recyclable, it is even better to reduce use of them in the first place. Putting cost and environmental issues aside, many people think that the flavor and texture of fresh-cooked dried beans is far superior to canned beans. (See page 22 for methods of cooking beans from dried.)

Converting recipes from dried to fresh and vice versa

It is really useful to be able to swap dried beans for canned beans in any recipe. Sometimes you may want to soak and cook your own beans, and sometimes you may only have time to reach for the can opener. An easy rule of thumb is that the weight of dried beans will double once cooked.

Converting from canned to dry weight

When a recipe calls for one 14 oz (400 g) can of cooked beans, you will find this contains about 8½ oz (240 g) of beans once drained. This means if you were starting from dried beans you would need to begin by soaking and cooking 4½ oz (120 g) dried beans.

Buying and storing dried beans

While one of the benefits of dried beans is that they have a very long shelf life, their age impacts on cooking time. Simply put, the older the bean, the longer the cooking. Flavor is also affected; younger beans will be more tasty. If possible, buy beans from the last season's harvest. In practice, its not always possible to know this for certain, so buy from a source that has a high turnover as their beans are likely to be fresher.

Once opened, dried beans and lentils will last for a year or so. Store in an airtight container and keep in a cool, dark, and dry place. And remember, the longer you store them, the longer they will take to cook, so adjust your cooking times accordingly.

Storing canned beans

Canned beans will last a very long time, possibly even several years—check the use-by date on your cans, you might be surprised at how long you can store them safely. For this reason, it's handy to have a few cans on hand for days when easy, speedy cooking is your number one priority.

COOKING DRIED BEANS

Beans are not as difficult to cook as you might think—it just takes a little time. Using a pressure cooker or a slow cooker can reduce the time you have to spend watching the stove.

All dried beans, as well as chickpeas (but not lentils or split peas) need soaking before cooking. The primary reason for this is to speed up the cooking process by rehydrating them first, so that they need to boil for far less time. The second (and some would say just as important) is to leach out some of the more indigestible carbohydrates that cause beans' somewhat infamous side effect. While soaking will by no means eliminate "bean gas," it should serve to reduce the symptoms. On this subject its also worth noting that over time, and by including beans regularly in your diet, you should find that any unwanted symptoms lessen.

There are two ways to soak beans, either a slow soak or a fast soak. Quick soaking is great for days when you have forgotten to get the beans soaking but it may result in bean skins that are more prone to wrinkle and cracking than a long, slow soak. So if appearance is as important as taste then it's better to get prepared ahead and go for the long soak method.

SOAKING METHODS

Slow soak method

1 Tip the beans into a sieve and rinse well under cold running water to remove any grit.

2 Pour into a large bowl and cover generously with cold water. Set aside for a minimum of 8 hours. Overnight will not hurt.

Quick soak method

1 Tip the beans into a sieve and rinse well under running water.

2 Add the beans to a pan and cover generously with cold water. Bring to the boil and cook rapidly for 2 minutes.

3 Remove the beans from the heat and set aside to soak in the cooking water for an hour before draining and rinsing.

Cooking the beans

Whichever soaking method you choose, rinse the beans again before adding to a large saucepan. Never be tempted to cook them in their soaking water, otherwise those gas-inducing carbohydrates will go straight into the pot and back into your beans.

Set over a medium-high heat and bring up to the boil, reduce to a steady simmer and cook until tender to the bite, skimming off and discarding any foam as it rises to the surface. A teaspoon of oil added to the cooking water will reduce the level of foam the beans produce. Do not add any salt during cooking as it can harden the skins.

Note Cooking time will depend on the variety of bean—some cook far more quickly than others. It is very difficult to be precise about cooking times as various factors will influence this—the age and dryness, soaking time, size and variety—even the altitude of your kitchen can affect cooking time.

Cooking particular weights

Dried beans can be cooked in bulk or as required to replace the canned beans in the recipes. The table on the right gives rough equivalent measurements.

TYPE OF BEANS	EQUIVALENT WEIGHTS
DRIED beans	4¼ oz (120 g)
CANNED beans [Drained weight]	14 oz (400 g) [8½ oz / 240 g]
FRESH beans	8½ oz (240 g)

COOKING BEANS IN A PRESSURE COOKER

Beans can be cooked with great speed in a pressure cooker, a big advantage; this method also reduces energy consumption from lengthy cooking times. The biggest disadvantage to pressure cooking is that you can't see what's going on and you can't test the beans for doneness while they are cooking. This makes timing a little tricky because, as mentioned on the previous page, cooking times for beans can vary with age.

It is also possible to cook beans in a pressure cooker without soaking. However, just as with the quick-soak method for conventional boiling, the skins are more prone to cracking than if they had a long soak beforehand, and of course you don't get the chance to soak away those indigestible carbohydrates either. So if you have time, it pays to soak beforehand even if you plan to cook in a pressure cooker.

It's worth noting that, as pressure cooking is so quick, it's really worth using a digital timer to time your cooking accurately. It's very easy to lose track of a few minutes, ending up with overcooked beans.

Pressure cooking method

1 Add the beans to a sieve and rinse well under running water. Soak as on page 22 using either the slow or fast soak method.

2 Tip the beans into your pressure cooker and cover generously with cold water. Never fill more than half full, including the water level. If the pan is too full there is a chance that the water will bubble up into the pressure release valve, risking a blockage. Add a teaspoon of oil to reduce the production of foam when the beans are cooking, and minimizing the chance of any froth blocking the pressure release valve.

3 Set the cooker on the hob and bring up to high pressure. Begin timing (using the table opposite as a guide) only once high pressure has been reached.

Bean cooking times

The table on the opposite page gives a rough guide to cooking the most common dried bean types (all times refer to pre-soaked beans with the exception of lentils, which do not need soaking).

Quesadillas

These delicious black-eyed peas could be bulk-cooked in advance, frozen, and added to the recipe like canned beans (see page 107).

TYPE OF BEANS	CONVENTIONAL BOILING	PRESSURE COOKER (AT 12 LBS PRESSURE)
Adzuki beans	30–45 minutes	6 minutes
Black beans	1–1¼ hours	8 minutes
Chickpeas	1–1½ hours	10 minutes
Butter beans	30–45 minutes	not recommended
Cranberry beans	1–1½ hours	10 minutes
Flageolet beans	1–1¼ hours	8 minutes
Navy beans	1–1½ hours	10 minutes
Pinto beans	1–1¼ hours	8 minutes
Cannellini	1–1½ hours	10 minutes
Puy lentils	15–20 minutes	not recommended
Red lentils	15–20 minutes	not recommended
Green lentils	15–20 minutes	not recommended
Brown lentils	15–20 minutes	not recommended

Note on pressure cooking times Pressure cooking given as 12 pounds pressure. For a pressure cooker of 15 pounds pressure, reduce times by a further 2 minutes.

USING A CROCK-POT OR SLOW COOKER TO COOK BEANS

Pre-soaked beans will take anything from 4-6 hours to become soft in a slow cooker on a high setting. Unsoaked beans will take significantly longer, another 3–4 hours, depending on age, type, and dryness of the bean. A low setting will produce delicious results but will take a much longer time. Pre-soaked beans may take around 10–12 hours, but again the exact timings vary and are specific to your bag of beans.

Please note, for safety, red kidney beans should not be added to a slow cooker or Crock-Pot unless they have been previously boiled rapidly for 10 minutes (see below).

Cooking kidney beans safely

Kidney beans contain toxins that can give you symptoms of food poisoning if they are not cooked properly. Never eat raw kidney beans. When cooking them from dry, it is really important that they are boiled hard and fast for 10 minutes at the start of the cooking process. Then you can turn them down to a simmer until they are soft.

Cooking butter beans

Butter beans are trickier than most to cook from dried. They often turn from hard and crunchy to overcooked and mushy in seconds, so it is crucial to get the timing just right. This is particularly true with pressure-cooking, when you can't see what is going on under the lid.

Bulk rewards

Some recipes in the book are particularly adapted to cooking in bulk. Make twice as much of this pilaki, then freeze in portions to eat later (see page 97).

STORING BEANS

Beans seem to be specially designed for easy storing—dry, freeze, or can them, and they still taste great. Once made, the recipes can also usually be stored to provide an extra dinner or lunch at a later date.

Storing and freezing cooked beans

Once dried beans are cooked, or canned beans are opened, drained and rinsed, they will keep well in the refrigerator stored in a covered container for several days. Cooked beans also freeze very well so if you are cooking a batch from dry its worthwhile cooking double what you need and freezing half for an easy meal at a later date. Simply pack into containers or freezer bags, seal tightly, and label, then freeze for up to 6 months. Either defrost overnight in the fridge, or for a couple of hours or so at room temperature. By freezing cooked beans you will suddenly have pretty much instant access to all the recipes in this book without the need to pre-plan on soaking time. However, if you use frozen beans, you cannot freeze leftovers.

Batch-cooking bean recipes

Many of these recipes make great leftovers, and the majority of bean recipes can be safely reheated once with no health issues. If you are planning to use leftovers the following day, to take into work for example, then simply ensure the finished recipe is cooled as quickly as possible before refrigerating. Speed up the cooling process by spreading the leftovers out—a wide dish will have a much larger surface area, thus speeding up cooling, than a tall, deep dish. Cooked beans in recipes will keep, covered and refrigerated, for up to 3 days.

Doubling up and scaling down

Most of the recipes in this book, unless otherwise stated, are designed to serve four people. For convenience, the recipes have been designed to use either one or two full-sized cans of cooked beans. The majority of recipes can be doubled up to feed more, and many could be halved if you are only feeding two. But as bean dishes store so well, it often makes sense to cook a full-sized recipe for an easy meal another day.

Freezing tip

Cook a large batch of beans from dried one weekend, when you have plenty of time. Instead of freezing in one bulk container, store the beans in individual can-sized portions, the same weight required for each recipe. Remember: A 14 oz (400 g) can of beans— drained and ready to use—is the same as 8½ oz (240 g) of cooked beans. That's 1⅓ measuring cups.

EASY EVERYDAY BEANS

With after-work eating in mind, dishes in this chapter are quick to make and suited to the tastes of the whole family. Many of the meals are suited to batch cooking and freezing in advance.

SERVES 4 | *One serving shown*

PREP 40 mins, including soaking

COOK 15 mins

This iconic Jamaican dish is normally served as a side to fiery jerk chicken, but it's also nutritious enough to eat on its own, perhaps with a crisp mixed salad.

Coconut rice and peas

INGREDIENTS

1²/₃ cups (10¹/₂ oz/300 g) long grain white rice

1 x 14 oz (400 ml) can coconut milk

1 scant cup (200 ml) water

1 tsp allspice berries, or ¹/₂ tsp ground allspice

1 tbsp dried thyme

1 tsp dried oregano

1 tsp dried chili flakes

1 x 14 oz (400 g) can black beans, drained and rinsed

Salt and freshly ground black pepper

METHOD

1 Place the rice, coconut milk, water, allspice, thyme, oregano, and chili into a medium-sized saucepan with a tight-fitting lid. Stir well and leave to soak for 30 minutes.

2 Add the black beans, stir, remove the lid, and set over a medium heat. Bring to the boil, replace the lid tightly, and boil for exactly 1 minute. Turn off the heat and leave, covered and undisturbed, for a further 13 minutes.

3 Once the rice has finished cooking, remove the lid and lightly fluff with a fork. Season to taste.

Thai-style yellow rice and beans

Replace the Jamaican herbs and spices with a Thai inspired mix—stir the following through the rice prior to soaking: 1 teaspoon ground turmeric powder, 2 lemongrass stalks, cut in half lengthwise and bruised with the flat of large knife, 8 Kaffir lime leaves, and 1 tablespoon grated fresh root ginger. Once the rice has cooked, remove the lemongrass stalks and stir through a handful of roughly chopped fresh cilantro.

Try other fish

You can also make these fishcakes with canned tuna, smoked salmon, or crab, simply substitute equal weights.

SERVES 4 | *One serving shown*

PREP 30 mins, plus 1 hour chilling

COOK 15–20 mins

Bean fishcakes are quick to make and more nutritious than potato versions. They also freeze really well, so why not make double and save half for next week.

Bean and smoked haddock fishcakes   F

INGREDIENTS

10¹/₂ oz (300 g) smoked haddock fillets

1 cup (240 ml) milk, or just enough to cover the fish

2 x 14 oz (400 g) cans white beans (such as cannellini or butter beans), drained and rinsed

2 scallions, finely chopped

1 tbsp fresh parsley, chopped

Pinch of grated nutmeg

Salt and freshly ground black pepper

Zest of half a lemon

Flour to dust the work surface

1 egg, lightly beaten

2 tbsp breadcrumbs

2 tbsp vegetable oil

METHOD

1 Place the haddock in a deep skillet and add enough milk to cover. Cover with a lid, bring up to a simmer, and cook for 5 minutes. Remove from the heat and leave to stand for 3 minutes. Remove the fish, reserving the cooking liquor, and set aside to cool. Once cool enough to handle, flake the fish, removing any stray bones.

2 In a large bowl place the beans, scallions, parsley, nutmeg, salt, pepper, and lemon zest, and puree with a handheld stick blender. Add the fish to the bean mixture and pulse to blend without completely pureeing the fish. Alternatively, process the beans, vegetables, and seasoning in a food processor, and stir the fish in with a spoon. Add a splash of the reserved milk to loosen and bind the mixture together.

3 Working on a floured surface, form the mixture into 8 equal-sized balls and flatten into patties. Dip each floured fishcake into the beaten egg and then into the breadcrumbs so that they are well coated. Place in the refrigerator to set for at least an hour.

4 Heat the oil in a large skillet and cook the fishcakes for 5–7 minutes on each side until golden and crispy.

SERVING SUGGESTION: Try the fishcakes for a light lunch with leafy salad and tartar sauce.

Cheese-filled fishcakes

Take each ball of fishcake mixture and make two patties, each 2¼ in (6 cm) in diameter, place 1½ teaspoons of garlic or herb cream cheese in the center of one patty and then place the second one on top. Seal around the edges by pressing before coating the fishcakes as above.

This easy bean curry recipe takes only minutes to throw together, so it's ideal for mid-week dinners. To make a dish that remains gluten-free, serve with brown rice.

Thai chickpea and spring green curry

Curry is gluten-free; use vegan curry paste

INGREDIENTS

2 tbsp vegetable oil

6 shallots, peeled and chopped

2 cloves garlic, minced

1 x 14 oz (400 ml) can coconut milk

1 scant cup (200 ml) water

2–3 tbsp Thai red curry paste (to taste)

2 tbsp light soy sauce

1 tsp sugar (white or brown)

2 x 14 oz (400 g) cans chickpeas, drained and rinsed

2 large heads of spring greens (or other dark green cabbage), finely sliced (9 oz/250 g prepared weight)

1 bunch cilantro, roughly chopped

Salt and freshly ground black pepper

METHOD

1 Heat the oil in a large saucepan and fry the shallots over a medium heat for around 5 minutes until soft and lightly colored. Add the garlic and fry for a further minute before pouring in the coconut milk and the water, stirring well to mix.

2 Stir through the curry paste, soy sauce, sugar, and chickpeas. Bring to the boil, cover with a lid and simmer steadily for 10 minutes.

3 Add the greens, stirring well to coat in the sauce. Replace the lid and cook for a further 5–8 minutes, or until the greens are tender but with a little bite.

4 Stir through the cilantro and season to taste.

SERVING SUGGESTION: Pair with egg noodles or rice.

Thai shrimp, tomato, and chickpea curry

For a slightly sweeter curry, simmer a handful of halved cherry tomatoes along with the chickpeas. Add 7 oz (200 g) of raw shrimp along with the spring greens, making sure they are pink and cooked all the way through before serving.

Frozen fresh

Peas, broad beans, and soy beans suffer very little for being frozen. They often have more vitamins and minerals than fresh as they are preserved at their absolute peak.

SERVES 4 | *One serving shown*

PREP 15 mins

COOK 30 mins

The butter stirred through just before serving adds a lovely richness to this otherwise super-healthy dish—simply leave it out if you prefer.

Fresh-bean pilaf with caramelized shallots and herbs

F ✹ ★ V

Pilaf is vegetarian; vegan if butter omitted

INGREDIENTS

4 tbsp olive oil

14 oz (400 g) shallots, finely sliced

3 cloves garlic, crushed

1¹/₃ cups (9 oz/250 g) basmati rice

2 cups (480 ml) hot vegetable stock

1 cup (7 oz/200 g) soy beans, fresh or frozen

1 cup (7 oz/200 g) baby broad beans, fresh or frozen

1 cup (7 oz/200 g) French beans, cut into bite-sized pieces

1 small bunch of fresh flat-leaf parsley, chopped

1 small bunch of fresh dill, chopped

1 small bunch of fresh chives, chopped

2 tbsp butter

Salt and freshly ground black pepper

METHOD

1 Heat the oil in a wide, deep saucepan and fry the shallots over a medium heat, stirring occasionally until crisped but not burned. Once caramelized, use a slotted spoon to transfer to a plate lined with paper towels. Set aside to drain.

2 Add the garlic to the pan and stir until the aroma is released—just a few seconds or so. Add the rice, stirring well to coat each grain in the oil. Pour in the stock, stir, and bring to the boil. Cover either with a tight-fitting lid or tightly tucked piece of foil. Simmer over a very low heat for 15 minutes.

3 While the rice is cooking blanch the beans; plunge them into boiling water and simmer for 4–5 minutes. Drain and set aside.

4 Remove the lid from the rice, stirring well if it has stuck a little to the base, and add the cooked beans, herbs, and shallots. Stir through the butter, and season to taste. Serve immediately.

SERVING SUGGESTION: Serve up with a slice of grilled salmon and fresh cut lemon wedges.

Spicy mixed-bean pilaf

For a protein-rich vegetarian main course, replace one of the fresh bean varieties with a drained and rinsed 14 oz (400 g) can of butter or cannellini beans. Add a little chopped fresh or dried chili to spice it up.

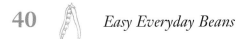
SERVES 4 | *Two servings shown*

PREP 10 mins

COOK 45 mins

A deliciously smooth and creamy soup drizzled with a tasty pesto sauce is a perfect starter or quick main served with lots of herby bread.

Creamy white bean soup with walnut and tarragon pesto

Soup is gluten-free; vegan if butter omitted

FOR THE SOUP

2 onions, chopped

1 tbsp olive oil

½ stick (2 oz/50 g) unsalted butter

4 cloves garlic, crushed

2 x 14 oz (400 g) cans cannellini beans, drained and rinsed

4 cups (1 l) vegetable stock

Salt and freshly ground black pepper

FOR THE PESTO

1 bunch fresh tarragon, leaves and fine stalks, roughly chopped

1 clove garlic, chopped

½ cup (2½ oz/65 g) chopped walnuts

¼ cup (50 ml) extra virgin olive oil

1 to 2 tbsp white wine vinegar

Salt and freshly ground black pepper

METHOD

1 To make the soup, gently sweat the onions in the olive oil and butter over a low heat until the onions are really soft but not colored at all. The longer and more slowly you can do this for the sweeter the soup will be, it will take at least 30 minutes.

2 Add the garlic and cook for a further couple of minutes before tipping in the beans and pouring over the stock. Simmer for 5 minutes then puree until completely smooth, either with a stick blender in the pan or by pouring into a food blender. Season to taste with salt and freshly ground black pepper.

3 To make the pesto, add all the ingredients to a food processor until blended to a smooth paste. Season to taste with salt and freshly ground black pepper.

SERVING SUGGESTION: Serve the soup with a little of the pesto drizzled over the top and some breadsticks for dipping.

Tomato twist

For the soup, replace 1 can of beans with a can of cranberry (borlotti) beans. Make a tomato pesto by blending the following ingredients: 1 cup (3½ oz/100 g) sun-dried tomatoes, drained and roughly chopped (reserve oil); 1 clove garlic, chopped; ½ cup (2½ oz/65 g) almonds; ¼ cup (50 ml) extra virgin olive oil (or the reserved tomato oil); 1 to 2 tbsp white wine vinegar; salt and freshly ground black pepper.

Meatless Mondays

For a hearty lunch, this is great served at room temperature with a spoon of hummus or Greek yogurt mixed with a little crushed garlic.

SERVES 4 | *Two servings shown*

PREP 30 mins

COOK 30–35 mins

Mujaddara is a deliciously simple Middle Eastern dish of rice and lentils topped with caramelized onions—a superb vegetarian dish that's just bursting with flavor.

Mujaddara with halloumi

INGREDIENTS

1¹/₃ cups (9 oz/250 g) dried green lentils

1 scant cup (200 ml) vegetable oil for frying

3 large onions, finely sliced

2 tbsp coriander seeds

1 tbsp cumin seeds

1¹/₃ cups (9 oz/250 g) basmati rice

1 tsp ground turmeric

1 tsp ground allspice

1 tsp ground cinnamon

1 tsp dried chili flakes (optional)

1²/₃ cups (400 ml) vegetable stock

Olive oil, for brushing

Salt and freshly ground black pepper

1 lb (450 g) halloumi cheese, cut into ¹/₄ in (7 mm) slices

1 small bunch cilantro, chopped

METHOD

1 Put the lentils in a small saucepan and cover with cold water. Bring to the boil and simmer rapidly for 10–12 minutes until they are just tender but with plenty of bite. Drain and set aside.

2 Meanwhile, heat the oil in a large, deep skillet until smoking hot. Drop in a piece of onion—it should sizzle instantly if the oil is hot enough. Fry the onion in 3 batches until crisp and golden, stirring occasionally, for about 5–7 minutes per batch. Using a slotted spoon, transfer to a bowl lined with paper towels. Set aside to drain and continue.

3 Once all the onions are cooked, discard all but a tablespoon of oil from the skillet. Add the coriander and cumin seeds and fry for a minute or two until toasted and fragrant. Tip in the rice and the cooked lentils, and stir well to coat in the toasted spices, then add the turmeric, allspice, cinnamon, and chili (if using). Pour in the stock, season, and bring to the boil. Reduce the heat, cover with a tight-fitting lid or tightly tucked piece of foil and simmer gently for 12 minutes. Turn off the heat and leave, covered and undisturbed, for a further 10 minutes.

4 While the rice is resting, heat a grill pan until smoking hot. Brush the halloumi lightly with olive oil and cook on both sides until crisp.

5 Fold through the cilantro and half the fried onions and tip into a serving dish. Sprinkle over the rest of the onions and top with the halloumi slices.

Mujaddara with spiced lamb

Take 7 oz (200 g) ground beef or lamb and fry in a skillet over a high heat, breaking it up with a spoon as it starts to cook. Add a teaspoon of cumin seeds, along with half a teaspoon each of ground cinnamon, and chili flakes. Keep frying until the meat has separated into crisp golden strands. Season with a little salt and sprinkle over the rice just before serving.

SERVES 4 | *One serving shown*

PREP 10 mins

COOK 45 mins

Rich, smoky bean chili is the ideal accompaniment to tacos or fajitas—extra fun with guacamole, salsa, grated cheese, and soured cream.

Kidney bean and mixed bell pepper chili

Chili is vegan if served plain

INGREDIENTS

3 tbsp vegetable oil

1 large onion, chopped

4 cloves garlic, finely chopped

2 red chilies, deseeded and chopped

½ tsp chili powder (optional)

1 tsp ground cumin

1 tsp ground coriander

1 tsp paprika

3 bell peppers (different colors), chopped into ½ in (1 cm) cubes

2 x 14 oz (400 g) cans kidney beans, drained and rinsed

1 x 14 oz (400 g) can chopped tomatoes

1 tsp brown sugar

Salt and freshly ground black pepper

METHOD

1 Heat the oil in a large saucepan and add the onion. Cook until it is soft and starting to caramelize, about 15 minutes on a high heat, stirring often to stop it burning.

2 Add the garlic, chopped chili, and spices and stir for another minute. Then add the peppers and stir them to coat with the spices.

3 Pour in the beans and tomatoes and stir through the sugar. Bring up to the boil and simmer, uncovered, for 20 minutes until thick and rich. Taste, season, and add a little more sugar if needed.

SERVING SUGGESTION: Sprinkle with grated cheese and a little chopped fresh cilantro, and scoop up the chili with nacho chips.

Beef chili

Make beef chili by adding either 14 oz (400 g) ground beef with the onions (brown the meat well before adding the other ingredients) or 10½ oz (300 g) leftover roasted beef, chopped into cubes. Omit two of the bell peppers. Cook the dish for at least an additional 20 minutes so that the meat is really tender. For a richer flavor, add 1–2 oz (30–55 g) of grated bittersweet chocolate to the dish as it is simmering— it is best to use a chocolate with at least 70 percent cocoa solids.

SERVES 4 | *One serving shown*

PREP 10 mins

COOK 55 mins

These burgers are fantastic served either with salad, or as a classic burger in a bun. Why not try them on the barbecue?

Spiced bean burgers

F V V

FOR THE BURGERS

1 medium head of cauliflower, chopped into small florets

3 tbsp olive oil

2 tbsp barbecue spice blend or seasoning

2 cloves garlic, finely sliced

1 x 14 oz (400 g) can butter beans, drained and rinsed

Juice of half a lemon, or to taste

1 handful of fresh cilantro, finely chopped

Salt and freshly ground black pepper

$^1/_4$ cup (1 oz/30 g) breadcrumbs

2 tbsp vegetable oil

FOR THE RELISH

1 large carrot, peeled and finely diced or grated

$^1/_2$ cup (110 ml) orange juice

1 to 3 red chilies, chopped, to taste

2 cloves garlic, crushed

$^1/_3$ cup (2 oz/55 g) canned sweet corn

1 ripe tomato, chopped

2 tbsp brown sugar

1 tbsp white wine or cider vinegar

2 tbsp cilantro, chopped

Salt and freshly ground black pepper

METHOD

1 Preheat the oven to 400°F (200°C/gas mark 6). To make the relish: place the carrots and orange juice in a saucepan, along with the chili, garlic, tomatoes, and and bring to the boil. Simmer until the carrots are very soft. Add the sweet corn, tomatoes, sugar, and vinegar, and stir well. Leave to cool, then add the cilantro and seasoning.

2 To make the burgers: place the cauliflower in a roasting pan with half the olive oil, the spices, and garlic. Mix, then bake for 30 minutes, turning once.

3 Using a hand blender or food processor, blend together the butter beans, the lemon juice, and half of the roast cauliflower until fairly smooth. Add the rest of the cauliflower and the cilantro and mix well. Taste the burger mix, add lemon juice, and season as needed.

4 Form the mixture into four equal-sized patties. Drizzle each with olive oil. Scatter the breadcrumbs on a plate and press the burgers into the breadcrumbs so that there is an even, thick coating. Heat a large skillet and add the oil. Fry the burgers for 5 minutes on each side until golden and crispy.

SERVING SUGGESTION: Serve in a ciabatta bun with some salad leaves and slices of tomato with the relish on the side.

Mexican-inspired kidney bean and squash burgers

Use canned kidney beans in place of butter beans. Replace the barbecue seasoning with a Mexican spice blend, plus a chopped red chili, and 2 chopped scallions. Replace the cauliflower with squash: toss 10 oz (300 g) peeled and cubed squash in a little oil, and bake in a hot oven for 30–40 minutes until soft. Blend this with the beans and then form and cook the burgers as above.

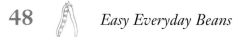

SERVES 4	*Two servings shown*
PREP 20 mins, plus marinating
COOK 1 hour 20 mins

This hot and spicy casserole is great served with plain rice—perfect for warming you up on a cold evening.

Jamaican red bean, spiced chicken, and sweet potato casserole

INGREDIENTS

2 tsp ground allspice

2 tsp ground cinnamon

2 tsp sweet paprika

2 tsp thyme (fresh or dried)

2 tbsp dark brown sugar

1 tsp salt

2 lb 2 oz (1 kg) chicken thighs and drumsticks (skin left on)

2 tbsp vegetable oil

2 large onions, finely sliced

4 cloves garlic, chopped

1 hot red chili, chopped

1 red bell pepper, chopped into 1 in (2.5 cm) chunks

2 medium sweet potatoes, peeled and chopped into 1 in (2.5 cm) cubes

1 tbsp tomato puree

1 x 14 oz (400 g) can kidney beans, drained and rinsed

6 scallions, sliced (white and green parts)

Salt and freshly ground black pepper

METHOD

1 Mix together the spices, sugar, and salt and sprinkle half over the chicken pieces. Drizzle with about half the oil and rub the spices thoroughly into the chicken. Leave to marinate for 10–20 minutes (or up to a day in the refrigerator).

2 Heat a large skillet and add the rest of the oil. Fry the chicken on a high heat until it is well browned all over, about 5–10 minutes on each side. Transfer the chicken to an ovenproof casserole dish. Preheat the oven to 400°F (200°C/gas mark 6).

3 Add the onions to the skillet and cook until soft but not colored, about 10 minutes. Then add the garlic, chili, and the rest of the spice mix, and stir-fry for 2 minutes. Add the bell pepper, sweet potato, and tomato puree and cook for 5 minutes. Finally, add the kidney beans and scallions and stir together.

4 Add the vegetable mixture to the chicken in the casserole dish and stir well, adding 1¼ cup (300 ml) of water. Cover with a tight-fitting lid or tightly tucked piece of foil and bake in the oven for 1 hour. Remove the lid or foil and taste, adding a little more salt and pepper as necessary.

SERVING SUGGESTION: Garnish with chopped fresh cilantro and fresh lime wedges.

Vegetarian red bean casserole with halloumi

Omit the chicken and make the vegetable and bean dish as above—it will only take 30 minutes to cook in the oven. Before serving, heat a grill pan with a splash of oil and when hot, add 2 thick slices of halloumi cheese per person, and cook on both sides. When crisp, cut into cubes, and sprinkle over the casserole to serve.

SERVES 4 | *One serving shown*

PREP 15 mins

COOK 50 mins

These spiced lentils are great served with fluffy naan bread for a warming, healthy meal.

Spiced green lentils and spinach with cilantro yogurt

The lentils are gluten-free if served plain

INGREDIENTS

2 large onions, red or white, chopped

2 tbsp vegetable oil

1 tbsp cumin seeds

1 tbsp nigella (black onion) seeds

1 tbsp ground coriander

1 tsp dried chili flakes

1 tsp ground turmeric

½ tsp ground cinnamon

3 cloves garlic, minced

2 in (4 cm) piece fresh root ginger, peeled and grated

1 cup (7 oz/200 g) dried green lentils

4 cups (1 l) vegetable stock

9 cups (14 oz/400 g) fresh spinach, washed and shaken dry

Salt and freshly ground black pepper

FOR THE CILANTRO YOGURT

4–6 tbsp plain yogurt (full or half fat)

1 small bunch of cilantro, finely chopped

Salt and freshly ground black pepper

METHOD

1 Take a large pan with a tight-fitting lid and gently sweat the onions in the oil, uncovered, for 15 minutes until soft and lightly caramelized. Add the dry spices, garlic, and grated ginger and fry for a minute or two until their aromas waft up from the pan.

2 Add the lentils, pour in the stock, and bring to the boil. Reduce the heat and cook uncovered at a steady simmer until the lentils are soft but not collapsing, about 25–30 minutes. Add a little more water toward the end of cooking if they are getting a little dry.

3 Add the spinach to the pan, packing it into a layer over the lentils. Cover tightly with a lid and allow it to wilt for 3 minutes, then gently fold through the lentils. Depending on the size of your pan you may need to add half the spinach at a time, wilting the first batch down before adding the second. Season to taste.

4 Make the yogurt dressing by mixing together the cilantro with the yogurt in a small bowl. Season to taste.

SERVING SUGGESTION: Serve with warm naan bread.

Red lentil dal

Use the same weight of red lentils, reducing the cooking time by 5 minutes or so. Make a cucumber raita to serve alongside in place of the cilantro yogurt—simply grate one third of a large cucumber, stir through the yogurt, and add chopped fresh mint leaves to taste.

SERVES 4–8 | *One serving shown*

PREP 5 mins, not including soaking

COOK 2 hours 20 mins – 2 hours 50 mins

This delicious dish tastes best when made with dried beans cooked slowly in the oven, but for a quicker meal, use canned navy beans and cook for 10–20 minutes on the stovetop.

Baked beans

Beans are gluten-free and vegan if served plain

INGREDIENTS

2 cups (7 oz/200 g) dried navy or cannellini beans, soaked overnight

2 bay leaves

1 small onion, halved

1 clove garlic

1 medium onion, very finely chopped

1 stick celery, very finely chopped

2 tbsp vegetable oil

1 clove garlic, minced

1 tablespoon tomato puree

1 x 14 oz (400 g) can chopped tomatoes

¼ cup (60 ml) water

2 tbsp dark brown sugar

1 tbsp red wine vinegar

Salt and freshly ground black pepper

METHOD

1 Drain the soaked beans and put in a large saucepan with the bay leaves, halved onion, and garlic. Add enough cold water to cover the beans by about 2 in (5 cm) and bring to the boil. Simmer until the beans are just soft, this could take 1–1½ hours depending on the beans. Drain the beans, and remove the bay leaves, onion, and garlic.

2 Preheat the oven to 325°F (170°C/gas mark 3). Heat a large heatproof casserole dish (if yours doesn't suit stovetop cooking, start in a saucepan and then transfer to a heatproof dish to bake). Fry the chopped onion and celery with the oil until soft, about 10 minutes. Add the garlic and tomato puree and fry for a few more minutes.

3 Add the tomatoes, water, sugar, vinegar, and season with ground black pepper, and simmer for 10 minutes.

4 Add the drained beans, stir, cover, and cook in the oven for 1 hour. Stir and check halfway through cooking to make sure the beans aren't drying out; if they are, add a splash of water. Add more sugar, vinegar, salt, and pepper to taste.

SERVING SUGGESTION: Top a piece of buttered toast with the beans.

Boston beans

Cook 12 oz (350 g) cubed belly pork or bacon with the chopped onions and celery, and add 2 tablespoons molasses and 1 teaspoon mustard powder with the garlic and tomato puree. Increase the baking time to 2–3 hours. Check and stir regularly, and add more water if the beans are drying out.

BEAN FEASTS

Made to impress, these bean dishes have been designed with feasting in mind: dinner parties, large family get-togethers, and celebrations. If you are planning a party, also check out the dips and snacks in chapter four.

Make it dairy free

Butter adds a lovely richness but for a dairy-free version, replace it with an extra tablespoon of olive oil.

SERVES 4 as a starter | *One to two servings shown*

PREP 5 mins

COOK 25 mins

This delicious and intensely savory bean topping makes a great dinner party starter served on crisp, toasted ciabatta.

White bean, lemon, and anchovy bruschetta

INGREDIENTS

1 red onion, finely chopped

1 tbsp olive oil

¼ stick (25 g) butter

1 clove garlic, minced

1 x 14 oz (400 g) can white beans (such as cannellini or butter beans), drained and rinsed

Finely grated zest of a lemon

1 small can anchovy fillets (1 oz/30 g drained weight), chopped

1 tbsp chopped fresh flat-leaf parsley

Salt and freshly ground black pepper

1 loaf ciabatta bread, sliced and toasted

METHOD

1 In a medium saucepan, sweat the onion in the olive oil and butter for a good 15 minutes until soft and lightly caramelized. Add the garlic and fry for a further minute, taking care not to burn it.

2 Pour in the beans, and add the lemon zest and chopped anchovy and gently fry for a further 5 minutes. Using a potato masher, break up the beans into a rough paste.

3 Stir through the parsley and season to taste—you may not need any salt depending on how strong the anchovies are. Serve warm on top of sliced, toasted ciabatta bread.

SERVING SUGGESTION: Drizzle with olive oil just before serving.

White bean, rosemary, and sun-dried tomato

For a delicious vegetarian alternative, add a tablespoon of finely chopped rosemary leaves to the onion as it is sweating. Omit the lemon and anchovy and add 3 tbsp chopped sun-dried tomatoes along with the beans.

SERVES 4 as a starter, 2 as a light meal | *One serving shown*

PREP 10 mins

COOK 30 mins

Pale, interesting, and elegant, this warm salad packs a mighty Mediterranean punch, full of the sunshine flavors of olive oil, lemon, and oregano.

Butter beans with roasted fennel and feta

INGREDIENTS

2 heads fennel

2 tbsp olive oil

A pinch of dried chili flakes

Salt and freshly ground black pepper

1 x 14 oz (400 g) can butter beans, drained and rinsed

7 oz (200 g) feta cheese, roughly crumbled

FOR THE DRESSING

2 tbsp extra virgin olive oil

Juice of ½–1 lemon, to taste

1 tsp clear honey

1 tsp Dijon mustard

1 tsp dried oregano (or 2 tsp chopped fresh oregano if available)

Salt and freshly ground black pepper

METHOD

1 Preheat the oven to 350°F (180°C/gas mark 4). Slice each fennel head through the root into eight wedges. Tip into a roasting pan and toss in the olive oil. Sprinkle over the chili flakes and season with a little salt and pepper. Cover with foil and roast for 20 minutes, then remove the foil and cook for another 10 minutes until cooked through and lightly golden.

2 Toss the butter beans through the fennel in the roasting pan while it is still hot. Set aside while you make the dressing.

3 In a small bowl, whisk together the olive oil with the juice of half a lemon. Add the honey, mustard, and oregano and whisk until thick and creamy. Season to taste with salt and pepper and add a little more lemon juice to sharpen if necessary.

4 To serve, arrange the fennel and butter beans on plates and scatter over the crumbled feta. Drizzle a little of the dressing over each salad, garnish with fennel fronds, and serve while still warm.

Butter beans with balsamic roasted bell peppers

Use three sliced red bell peppers in place of the fennel, tossing in the oil and 2 tablespoons of balsamic vinegar. Roast, uncovered, for a reduced time of 20 minutes before continuing as above. Try using thyme or marjoram in place of the oregano in the dressing.

Crispy wontons

Make the wontons as described, right, but instead of cooking them in a saucepan, fry them in 1–2 tablespoons of sesame oil in a wok or large skillet. Fry until they are crispy on both sides—about 5 minutes. Just before serving, add a splash of water or stock—this helps to steam the wonton skins. Serve the crispy wontons with a small dish of dipping sauce.

SERVES 4 | *Two servings shown*

PREP 30 mins

COOK 10 mins

This soup contains handmade wonton parcels in a delicious, light broth. It makes a warming and unusual starter for four people.

Black bean and shrimp wonton soup

FOR THE WONTONS

³/₄ oz (20 g) salted black beans, or 4 tbsp black bean sauce

5 oz (150 g) shrimp, cooked and peeled

1 cup (30 g) shredded white cabbage

3 scallions, chopped

¹/₂ red bell pepper, finely chopped or grated

1¹/₄ in (3 cm) fresh root ginger, peeled and grated

1 tsp sesame oil

¹/₂ tsp + 1 tbsp cornstarch, plus extra for dusting

1 tsp soy sauce

16 wonton skins

2 tbsp water

FOR THE BROTH

4 cups (1 l) good-quality stock (chicken, fish, or vegetable)

4 scallions

1¹/₄ in (3 cm) fresh root ginger, peeled and julienned

1 tbsp soy sauce, or more to taste

Juice of half a lime or lemon

Small handful fresh cilantro

METHOD

1 To make the wontons: place the black beans or sauce, shrimp, cabbage, scallions, pepper, and root ginger in a food processor and briefly pulse so that the ingredients are all well chopped. Be careful not to overprocess or the filling will be too smooth—mince everything by hand with a knife if you prefer. Add the sesame oil, ¹/₂ teaspoon of cornstarch, and soy sauce and mix until the filling comes together so you can form balls. Divide the mixture into 16 walnut-sized balls.

2 Mix together the 1 tablespoon of cornstarch with 2 tablespoons water. Place a wonton skin on a clean surface and brush all around the edges generously with the cornstarch water. Place a ball of the filling in the middle and bring the wonton skin together so that the edges meet—you will either make a half-moon or a triangle depending on the shape of the skins. Squeeze around the edges so that the filling is sealed inside the skin: leave about ¹/₂ in (1 cm) of the edges free from filling to create a seal. Dip one of the points of the triangle or half-moon into the cornstarch water and pinch it together with the opposite point. Repeat with the rest of the skins and filling—place the finished wontons on a plate lightly covered with cornstarch to stop them from becoming sticky.

3 To make the soup: heat the broth ingredients—except the cilantro—together in a large saucepan, taste, and add more soy sauce, lime juice, or fresh root ginger if required. Add the wontons and simmer them for 3 minutes. They will float to the top when they are ready. Serve four wontons in each bowl of broth, and sprinkle with the cilantro.

Harissa paste

Harissa is a rich and very spicy paste made from dried chilies. Different brands can vary a lot in heat, so add a little at a time, to taste. You can always pass a little dish with extra harissa around for those who like extra heat.

This spicy, Moroccan tagine-style stew is great served with plenty of steamed couscous to soak up the delicious sauce.

SERVES 4

PREP 15 mins

COOK 1 hr 50 mins

Chickpea, lamb, and harissa stew

Stew is gluten-free if served plain

INGREDIENTS

2 tbsp olive oil

1 lb 5 oz (600 g) stewing lamb, cut into bite-sized pieces

2 onions, chopped

3 cloves garlic, crushed

2 tsp cumin seeds

1 tsp paprika

1 tsp ground ginger

1 tsp ground cinnamon

2 x 14 oz (400 g) cans chickpeas, drained and rinsed

1 x 14 oz (400 g) can chopped tomatoes

1²/₃ cups (400 ml) vegetable stock

Salt and freshly ground black pepper

1 to 3 tbsp harissa paste (to taste)

1 small bunch of cilantro, chopped

METHOD

1 Heat the oil until smoking hot in a heavy-based, large saucepan and sear the diced lamb in two batches until browned (about 5 minutes per batch). If you add too much meat to the pan, it will lower the temperature and the meat will sweat rather than brown.

2 Once browned, return all the meat to the pan, lower the heat to minimum and add the onions and fry for about 10 minutes until they are starting to soften and caramelize. Add the garlic and spices, and fry for just a minute before adding the chickpeas and tomatoes.

3 Pour in the stock and bring to the boil. Season with a little salt and pepper, cover with a lid, and simmer for an hour.

4 Remove the lid, stir in the harissa to taste and simmer, uncovered, for further 30 minutes until the sauce is thick and the lamb is tender. Taste to check the seasoning and sprinkle with the cilantro just before serving.

SERVING SUGGESTION: Spoon over fluffy couscous mixed with cilantro.

Butternut squash tagine

For a vegetarian version, chop a medium-sized butternut squash into bite-sized chunks. Heat the oil in a pan, add the squash, and fry over a high heat until it colors a little at the edges, about 10 minutes. Then proceed as in the recipe above but reduce the cooking time to an hour total, 30 minutes covered and 30 minutes uncovered.

SERVES 4 | *One serving shown*

PREP 10 mins, plus 30 mins soaking

COOK 20 mins

Heady with white wine and garlic, this Italian-style stew is rich and delightfully fragrant. Any mix of fresh mushrooms can be used.

Pinto bean and wild mushroom ragout

When served with vegetarian cheese

INGREDIENTS

1 cup (250 ml) boiling water

1 oz (30 g) dried porcini mushrooms

1³/₄ oz (50 g) unsalted butter

3 cloves garlic, sliced

1¹/₂ lb (700 g) mixed mushrooms, sliced

1 x 14 oz (400 g) can pinto beans, drained and rinsed

1 cup (250 ml) white wine

Salt and freshly ground black pepper

1 generous bunch of basil, roughly chopped

1 oz (30 g) freshly grated Parmesan

METHOD

1 Measure the boiling water into a heatproof jug and add the dried porcini. Set aside to soak for 30 minutes.

2 Ten minutes before the mushrooms have finished soaking, begin the stew. Melt the butter in a deep, wide skillet and sweat the garlic for a few minutes without burning. Add the sliced mushrooms and cook gently for about 10 minutes until soft. Add the pinto beans and pour in the porcini and their strained soaking water.

3 Pour in the wine, season well with salt and pepper, and simmer, partially covered, for around 10 minutes until the mushrooms are cooked, the beans soft, and the sauce slightly reduced.

4 Just before serving, stir through the basil and taste to check the seasoning. Serve in warmed bowls with the Parmesan scattered over.

SERVING SUGGESTION: Mix through cooked pasta for a hearty main course. Top with the Parmesan and a little extra chopped basil to garnish.

Pinto bean, sun-dried tomato, and Parma ham ragout

Add a handful of chopped sun-dried tomatoes with the mushrooms. Tear a few slices of Parma ham into bite-sized pieces and scatter over the ragout just before serving. Toast diced ciabatta with olive oil to make crisp croutons and scatter over just before serving, or serve with slices of garlic bread.

SERVES 4 | *One serving shown*

PREP 10 mins, plus 24 hours soaking

COOK 10 mins

This delicious Mediterranean fish dip is made with salt cod, also known as *bacalao* in Portuguese, or *baccala* in Spanish and Italian.

Salt cod and butter bean brandade

Brandade is gluten-free if served plain

INGREDIENTS

7 oz (200 g) salted cod

1 cup (250 ml) milk, or just enough to cover the fish

1 small onion, roughly chopped

1/2 tsp black peppercorns

2 bay leaves

1 x 14 oz (400 g) can butter beans, drained and rinsed

4 tbsp extra virgin olive oil

Juice of half a lemon, or to taste

METHOD

1 Begin the dish 24 hours before you want to serve it by putting the salted cod in a large bowl and totally submersing it in cold water. Soak in the refrigerator for 24 hours, changing the water a couple of times.

2 Rinse and drain the cod, and lay it in a saucepan. Pour over just enough milk to cover, and add the onion, peppercorns, and bay leaves. Cover with a lid or tightly tucked piece of foil and bring up to the boil. Simmer for 5 minutes or until the fish is just cooked. Remove carefully (reserve the cooking liquor) to a plate and allow to cool a little, just enough so you can flake the flesh, removing any bones.

3 Puree the butter beans in a food processor or with a stick blender, adding just enough of the fish cooking milk to loosen to a smooth paste.

4 Add the olive oil and lemon juice and process well to mix, then add the fish flakes and pulse until just mixed. Don't overprocess or the texture will become a little gluey. Transfer to a serving dish and drizzle over a little extra olive oil. Serve with crisp, hot toast.

SERVING SUGGESTION: Serve with thin and elegant melba toasts or on slices of cucumber to keep the recipe gluten-free.

Quick bean dip

Replace the salt cod with flaked, ready-cooked smoked mackerel, replacing the butter beans with pinto beans. You may need to add little extra olive oil to loosen the texture, or a spoon of crème fraîche for a creamy version. Use peppered smoked mackerel to make a lovely spicy dip.

Advance warning

Don't rush the soaking of the cod: it really does need 24 hours in cold water, so be sure to begin the recipe in plenty of time.

SERVES 4	
PREP 15 mins	
COOK 30 mins	

A Spanish-inspired fish stew, rich with saffron and smoked paprika—a great meal to serve at the table.

Catalan bean and fish stew

Stew is gluten-free if served plain

INGREDIENTS

5 tbsp olive oil

4 medium shallots, sliced

4 garlic cloves, sliced

14 oz (400 g) baby new potatoes, halved

¹/₂ cup (120 ml) dry sherry or dry white wine

1 tsp smoked paprika

2 sprigs of fresh thyme

2 bay leaves

A large pinch of saffron soaked in 1 tbsp boiling water for 10 minutes

2 cups (500 ml) fish stock

1 x 14 oz (400 g) can cannellini beans, drained and rinsed

1 x 14 oz (400 g) can butter beans, drained and rinsed

Salt and freshly ground black pepper

1 lb 2 oz (500 g) skinless white fish such as haddock, hake or bass, cut into bite-sized pieces

8 cherry tomatoes

A small bunch of flat-leaf parsley, chopped

7 oz (200 g) fresh mussels, scrubbed and rinsed in a few changes of water

A squeeze of lemon juice plus lemon wedges, to serve

METHOD

1 Heat 4 tablespoons of olive oil in a large saucepan and add the shallots. Fry over a medium heat until soft and slightly browned and then add the garlic. Stir for 2 minutes and then add the potatoes, sherry, smoked paprika, thyme, bay leaves, and saffron (including soaking water) and stir again for another couple of minutes.

2 Add the stock and cover with a tight fitting lid, or tightly fitted piece of foil, bring to the boil and simmer steadily until the potatoes are almost cooked—about 10 minutes. Stir in the beans and simmer for another couple of minutes. Season to taste with salt and pepper.

3 Add the fish, tomatoes and half of the parsley and gently simmer for 3 minutes or until the fish is almost cooked and then add the mussels. Place the lid on the saucepan for 2 minutes or until all of the mussels have opened. Discard any mussels that do not open; they are not safe to eat.

4 Serve drizzled with a little extra olive oil, a squeeze of lemon juice, and the rest of the parsley scattered on top. You can also serve extra lemon wedges alongside.

SERVING SUGGESTION: Provide plenty of rustic bread to soak up the sauce.

Catalan bean and chorizo stew

In place of the white fish, fry 7 oz (200 g) of thick-sliced chorizo with the garlic. Continue with the recipe as above. Use chicken stock instead of fish stock.

SERVES 4 | *One serving shown*

PREP 10 mins

COOK 40 mins

This thick soup is hearty enough to be served as a main course, specially served with a deliciously refreshing topping of avocado puree.

Black bean and corn soup

Vegan/vegetarian if made with vegetable stock; gluten-free if served plain

FOR THE SOUP

2 tbsp oil

1 onion, chopped

1 stick celery, finely chopped

2 cloves garlic, finely chopped

1 red chili, finely chopped

1 tsp ground cumin

1 tsp ground coriander

1 tsp dried chili flakes

2 x 14 oz (400 g) cans black beans, drained and rinsed

5 oz (140 g) sweet corn (frozen or canned)

Zest and juice of a lime

2¹/₂ cups (600 ml) stock (vegetable or beef)

2 large, ripe tomatoes or 10 cherry tomatoes, chopped

A handful of cilantro, chopped

Salt and freshly ground black pepper

METHOD

1 Heat the oil in a large saucepan and add the onion and celery, fry for 10–15 minutes or until they are soft and lightly caramelized. Add the garlic, chili, and spices and fry for 5 minutes.

2 Stir through the black beans, sweet corn, the zest of the lime, and half the juice, along with the stock. Bring to the boil and simmer for 15 minutes.

3 Transfer half of the soup to a bowl and blend to a smooth consistency with a stick blender. Combine the pureed beans with the rest of the soup, add the chopped tomatoes, and simmer for a further 5 minutes.

4 Meanwhile, make the avocado puree by removing the flesh from the avocado and mashing it until smooth with a fork. Add the garlic, lime juice, salt and pepper, and olive oil and taste, adding as much Tabasco as you like. Taste the soup and add salt, pepper, and lime juice to taste. Serve the soup with a spoonful of avocado puree and garnished with the chopped cilantro.

SERVING SUGGESTION: Serve up with triangles of lightly baked tortillas or flatbread and drizzled with soured cream.

Hearty soup

Add a large handful of pulled pork or leftover roasted beef, chopped, to the soup with the tomatoes, and continue cooking as above. Divide the soup between four bowls and top each with tortilla chips and grated cheese. Place under a hot broiler until the cheese is melted and then add the avocado puree and cilantro on top. Serve with a bowl of soured cream.

FOR THE AVOCADO PUREE

1 ripe avocado

1 clove garlic, finely chopped

Juice of half a lime

Salt and freshly ground black
  pepper

1 tbsp olive oil

A few drops of Tabasco sauce
  (to taste)

Use a tomato mix

This is even better when made with different varieties of tomatoes. Try a mixture of cherry, plum, heirloom, and beef tomatoes cut into similar-sized pieces for even cooking.

SERVES 4 | *One serving shown*

PREP 5 mins

COOK 30 mins

A wonderfully rich treat that makes the most of ripe summer tomatoes. Served with extra bread to soak up the sauce, this makes a lovely lunch made for sharing.

Italian-style baked cranberry beans

INGREDIENTS

1¼ cup (300 ml) heavy cream

2 tsp brown sugar

2 tbsp capers, drained, rinsed, and roughly chopped

2 cloves garlic, finely chopped

1 small bunch of basil, chopped

Salt and freshly ground black pepper

2 x 14 oz (400 g) cans cranberry beans, drained and rinsed

6 to 7 medium size, ripe tomatoes, quartered

FOR THE CROUTONS

Half a ciabatta loaf, torn into pieces

1 tbsp olive oil

METHOD

1 Preheat the oven to 400°F (200°C/gas mark 6). In a large bowl, mix together the cream, sugar, capers, garlic, and basil. Season well with salt and pepper.

2 Add the cranberry beans and tomatoes and stir to mix. Pour into a baking dish large enough for the tomatoes to spread in a shallow layer. Bake for 20 minutes until the tomatoes are soft and starting to color a little at the edges.

3 Meanwhile, spread out the ciabatta pieces on a baking tray and drizzle over the olive oil. Bake alongside the beans and tomatoes for 5–8 minutes until starting to crisp up.

4 Remove the tomatoes and croutons from the oven, sprinkle the croutons over the the baking dish and return to the oven for 10 more minutes. Allow to cool a little before serving.

Olive or anchovy flavored bake

Replace the capers with either 2 tablespoons of roughly chopped black olives or a small can of finely chopped anchovy fillets. Top the croutons with a handful of finely grated fresh Parmesan before returning the dish to the oven to finish baking. Alternatively, serve stirred through cooked pasta as a hearty main course.

SERVES 4 | *Two servings shown*

PREP 10 mins

COOK 45–55 mins

Make this recipe in a dish that can go from the stovetop to the oven, or make the tagine in a saucepan and transfer to an ovenproof dish before adding the eggs.

Navy bean and chard tagine with baked eggs

INGREDIENTS

2 tsp cumin seeds

2 tsp coriander seeds

1 tsp fennel seeds

1 tsp dried chili flakes

2 onions, sliced

3 tbsp olive oil

3 cloves garlic, crushed

2 x 14 oz (400 g) cans chopped tomatoes

2 x 14 oz (400 g) cans navy beans, drained and rinsed

Large bunch chard, leaves and stalks chopped

4 large eggs

Salt and freshly ground black pepper

METHOD

1 Dry-fry the spices, tip into a pestle and mortar, and roughly grind.

2 Pour the oil into a large, flameproof casserole dish and add the onions and ground spices. Gently sweat over a medium-low heat for 10–15 minutes until the onions soften and start to caramelize. Add the garlic and cook for a further minute before pouring in the tomatoes and navy beans. Bring to the boil and simmer steadily for around 15 minutes until the sauce is thick and rich.

3 Add the chopped chard and cover with a lid or tightly fitted piece of foil. Simmer for a further 5 minutes until the chard is almost tender but with a little bite.

4 Preheat the oven to 350°F (180°C/gas mark 4). Make four wells in the surface of the tagine and crack an egg into each. Season the surface with a little salt and freshly ground black pepper and bake in the oven until the eggs are cooked to your liking—around 15–20 minutes for set whites and runny yolks.

SERVING SUGGESTION: Cook this in individual dishes rather than one large dish, one egg on top of each dish.

Crunchy-top pie

Cook and mash 4 medium white potatoes with ¼ cup (50 ml) milk or cream. Carefully pipe or spoon on top of the dish before baking, and then top with a mixture of 1 cup (100 g) breadcrumbs and 1 cup (100 g) grated cheese. Cook for 15–20 minutes.

SERVES 4 as a starter, 2 as a light meal	
PREP 15 mins	
COOK 65–75 mins	

This is a tasty take on the the southern French classic, cassoulet. Gremolata is a punchy herb and garlic mixture to sprinkle over as you eat, adding a zesty freshness to every mouthful.

Flageolet and Toulouse sausage casserole with gremolata

Casserole is gluten-free if served plain; check sausages are gluten-free

INGREDIENTS

1 tbsp olive oil

6 Toulouse sausages (or other herby sausage)

2 onions, chopped

2 carrots, cut into chunks

1 head of fennel, sliced

3 cloves garlic, sliced

2 bay leaves, fresh or dried

1 tsp fennel seeds

2 x 14 oz (400 g) cans chopped tomatoes

1¼ cup (300 ml) vegetable or chicken stock

¾ cup (175 ml) red wine

2 x 14 oz (400 g) cans flageolet beans, drained and rinsed

Salt and freshly ground black pepper

FOR THE GREMOLATA

1 large garlic clove, minced

Finely grated zest of a lemon

A small bunch flat-leaf parsley, finely chopped

METHOD

1 Heat the oil in a large flameproof casserole dish and fry the sausages over a medium heat until golden-brown all over. Remove and set aside.

2 Reduce the heat to low and add the onions, carrots, and fennel, along with the garlic, bay leaves, and fennel seeds. Sweat gently for 10–15 minutes until softening and starting to caramelize.

3 Return the sausages to the casserole dish, and add the tomatoes, stock, and wine, bring to the boil and simmer, uncovered, for 40 minutes. Add the beans and simmer for a further 10 minutes, until the sauce is thick and rich and the vegetables are tender. Season to taste with salt and black pepper.

4 To make the gremolata: mix all the ingredients in a small bowl. Serve the casssoulet in deep bowls, allowing your guests to sprinkle the gremolata over the cassoulet as they eat.

SERVING SUGGESTION: Mop up the casserole juices with thick, crusty French bread.

Flageolet and chicken casserole

Replace the sausages with 4 large chicken thighs—simply brown them in the same way as the sausages and carry on as above. Try using 4–5 sticks of celery instead of the fennel.

BEANS TO GO

Beans make an excellent range of salads and snacks to take with you for lunch on the go or for lunch at work because they won't wilt or dry out if kept covered and cool.

SERVES 4 as a starter, 2 as a light meal | *One meal-size serving shown*
PREP 15 mins
COOK 25 mins

This salad can be served hot or cold—when served hot, the cheese will melt and form a sauce. It's fantastic tossed through cooked fettuccine or pappardelle pasta.

Puy lentils with Gorgonzola and sun-dried tomatoes

F ✦ ★ V

INGREDIENTS

7 oz (200 g) dried Puy lentils

1 shallot, finely diced

2 bay leaves

3 tbsp balsamic vinegar

3 tbsp olive oil

Salt and freshly ground black pepper

½ cup (1¾ oz/50 g) sun-dried tomatoes

1 cup (3½ oz/100 g) Gorgonzola cheese

1 handful basil leaves

1 tsp Dijon mustard

3½ cups (3½ oz/100 g) baby spinach leaves

METHOD

1 Place the lentils, shallot, and bay leaves in a medium saucepan and cover well with cold water. Bring to the boil and simmer until the lentils are soft, about 20 minutes. Drain, removing the bay leaf. Add 1 tbsp balsamic vinegar, 1 tbsp olive oil, and a little salt and pepper, and let stand for 5 minutes.

2 While the lentils are standing, chop the sun-dried tomatoes and Gorgonzola cheese into rough chunks, and tear the basil leaves into small strips.

3 In a small bowl, whisk the remaining balsamic vinegar with the mustard and add the remaining olive oil a little at a time until the dressing thickens. Taste and season with salt and pepper.

4 Place the lentils on a bed of spinach and scatter the sun-dried tomatoes and Gorgonzola over the top, garnish with the basil, and drizzle with the dressing.

Lentil-stuffed roasted vegetables

To make a great stuffing for roasted zucchini, bell peppers, or squash: prepare the lentils as above. Cut the vegetable in half lengthwise (removing the seeds if necessary), rub all over with olive oil and place in an oven preheated to 400°F (200°C/ gas mark 6) until cooked through. Zucchini will take 10 minutes, bell peppers will take 15–20 minutes, and squash will take 40–50 minutes. Fill the roasted vegetable with the Puy lentil mixture and return to the oven for 10 minutes until the cheese melts. Serve the roasted, stuffed vegetables on wilted baby spinach leaves.

SERVES 4 | *One serving shown*

PREP 10 mins

COOK 10 mins

Who can resist a salad with the works? If you have time or some leftover tuna steak, you can substitute grilled tuna steaks for the canned tuna.

Butter bean Niçoise salad

FOR THE DRESSING

3 tbsp olive oil

2 tbsp white wine vinegar

1 tsp Dijon mustard

1 tsp sugar

Salt and freshly ground black pepper

FOR THE SALAD

4 eggs

3 shallots, very finely sliced

2 x 14 oz (400 g) cans butter beans, drained and rinsed

1 x 7 oz (200 g) can sweet corn, drained

1 handful green or black olives

1 bunch of flat-leaf parsley, chopped

1 x 6 oz (170 g) can tuna, drained and flaked

METHOD

1 Make the dressing by whisking together all the ingredients in a small bowl. Season to taste with salt and pepper.

2 Place the eggs in a pan of cold water. Bring to the boil and boil for 5 minutes until just hard boiled. Drain, run under cold water to cool then peel and chop in half. Set aside.

3 In a larger bowl, toss together the shallots, beans, sweet corn, olives, and parsley. Pour in the dressing and mix well.

4 Arrange in a serving dish, scatter over the tuna flakes and egg halves.

Niçoise with cheese

Replace the tuna with 1 cup (7 oz/200 g) crumbled feta cheese or 1 cup (7 oz/200 g) torn mozzarella cheese. Serve on a bed of peppery rocket leaves. For a greener Niçoise, replace one of the cans of butter beans with 1$^{1}/_{2}$ cups (10$^{1}/_{2}$ oz/300 g) lightly cooked fresh green beans.

SERVES 4 | *One serving shown*

PREP 10 mins

COOK 30 mins

Roasting the vegetables with balsamic vinegar gives this dish a really intense flavor that will remind you of sunny days.

Navy bean and roasted vegetable salad with mozzarella

Salad is gluten-free if served plain

INGREDIENTS

4 tbsp olive oil

3 tbsp balsamic vinegar

1 tsp sugar

1 clove garlic, crushed

Salt and freshly ground black pepper

2 red bell peppers, deseeded and cut into strips

12 to 15 cherry tomatoes, halved

2 red onions, cut into wedges through the root

¹/₂ butternut squash, cut into ¹/₂ in (1 cm) cubes

2 x 14 oz (400 g) cans navy beans, drained and rinsed

2 tbsp capers, drained and roughly chopped

Small bunch basil, roughly chopped

2 balls fresh mozzarella, torn into bite-sized pieces

METHOD

1 Preheat the oven to 400°F (200°C/gas mark 6). In a small bowl, whisk together the olive oil, balsamic vinegar, sugar, and garlic. Season with a little salt and pepper.

2 Spread the vegetables out in a large roasting pan and pour over half the dressing, tossing well to mix. Roast for 30 minutes, turning once.

3 Remove the vegetables from the oven and stir through the beans, remaining dressing, capers, and basil and stir well to coat. Serve the salad with the mozzarella scattered on top.

SERVING SUGGESTION: The perfect lunch at work, combined with some focaccia bread.

Bean salad with honey-roasted salmon

In a small bowl, whisk together 1 tablespoon of clear honey with 1 crushed garlic clove and ¹/₂ teaspoon of smoked paprika. Spread over 2 salmon fillets and set aside to marinate. Lay the salmon on top of the roasting vegetables halfway through cooking time. To serve, flake the cooked salmon over the salad in place of the mozzarella.

SERVES 4 | *One serving shown*

PREP 30 mins, plus marinating

COOK 15 mins

Crisp and crunchy with a punchy dressing, this is a great lunchtime salad. You can use any long green beans— these are extra long "snake" beans.

Coconut chicken salad

FOR THE CHICKEN

4 small, skinless chicken breasts

1 scant cup (200 ml) coconut milk

1¹/₂ to 2 in (3 to 5 cm) piece fresh root ginger, peeled and grated

2 cloves garlic, crushed

1 tsp ground turmeric

2 to 3 red birds-eye chilies, finely chopped

Small bunch cilantro, leaves and fine stalks chopped

Salt and freshly ground black pepper

FOR THE SALAD

1¹/₂ cups (10¹/₂ oz/300 g) runner beans, chopped into bite-sized pieces

1¹/₂ cups (10¹/₂ oz/300 g) green beans or snake beans

2 green or yellow zucchini, finely sliced lengthwise

FOR THE DRESSING

2 tbsp sesame oil

Zest and juice of a large lime

1 red bird's eye chili, finely chopped

Small bunch cilantro, leaves chopped

1 to 2 tsp sugar, to taste

METHOD

1 Make two or three diagonal slashes in each chicken breast and lay in a shallow dish. Add the coconut milk, ginger, garlic, turmeric, chili, cilantro, and seasoning and mix thoroughly before rubbing all over the chicken. Cover and marinate in the refrigerator for at least 2 hours or overnight.

2 When you are ready to cook the chicken, preheat the oven to 400°F (200°C/gas mark 6). Place the chicken in a baking pan and roast for 12–15 minutes until cooked through. Allow to cool a little before cutting into ¹/₂ in (1 cm) slices.

3 Bring a pan of lightly salted water to the boil and cook the beans for 3 minutes. Add the zucchini ribbons and cook for a further minute before draining well and tipping into a mixing bowl.

4 Make the dressing by mixing all the ingredients together in a small bowl. Pour over the warm beans and zucchini and toss well to coat. Serve the salad warm or cold with the sliced chicken on top.

Mixed bean and tofu salad

For a vegan option, replace the chicken with half a block of drained, firm tofu. Dice the tofu into 1 in (2.5 cm) chunks before marinating. Bake for a little longer—30 minutes at 350°F (180°C/gas mark 4) or until the coating has crisped a little around the edges, but do not allow to blacken.

SERVES 4 | *Four servings shown*

PREP 5 mins, plus marinating

COOK 10 mins

This Spanish-inspired salad tastes best served at room temperature to allow the flavors to shine through, with plenty of fresh lemon to squeeze on top.

Lemon squid with parsley and white beans

INGREDIENTS

- 1 large squid, (about ³/₄ lb/ 350 g), cleaned and sliced into ¹/₄ in (5 mm) rings
- 3 tbsp extra virgin olive oil
- Zest and juice of a lemon
- 3 garlic cloves, crushed
- 1 tsp dried chili flakes (or to taste)
- 2 x 14 oz (400 g) cans white beans (such as cannellini or butter beans), drained and rinsed
- 4 large, ripe tomatoes, diced
- 1 small bunch flat-leaf parsley, chopped
- Salt and freshly ground black pepper

METHOD

1 Place the squid rings in a bowl and stir through the olive oil, lemon zest and juice, garlic, and chili flakes. Set aside to marinate in the refrigerator for 30 minutes.

2 Heat a skillet until very hot and add the marinated squid and all the juices. Stir-fry quickly until the squid has turned opaque and is cooked through—just a couple of minutes.

3 Add the beans, tomatoes, and parsley to the skillet, season well with salt and pepper and stir-fry for a further couple of minutes until the tomato just begins to soften. Remove from the heat and allow to cool to room temperature before serving.

Shrimp salad

Replace the squid with the same weight of raw jumbo shrimp, and marinate in flavors inspired by Asian cuisine: mix 1 tablespoon toasted sesame oil with 1 tablespoon light vegetable oil. Add 4 finely chopped scallions, 2 minced garlic cloves, a little finely grated fresh root ginger, the zest and juice of a lime, and a couple of finely chopped red bird's eye chilies. Replace the parsley with cilantro.

FOR THE SALAD

4 eggs, hard–boiled, peeled, and halved

1 lb 2 oz (500 g) new potatoes

1 cup (10¹/₂ oz/300 g) green beans, topped and tailed

1¹/₂ cups (5 oz/150 g) cabbage (white, Chinese, or spring greens), shredded

1 cup (2 oz/60 g) bean sprouts

Small bunch cilantro, chopped

1 red chili, finely chopped

2 cups (2 oz/60 g) prawn crackers or cassava chips, to serve

FOR THE PEANUT SAUCE

2 red chilies, chopped

2 cloves garlic

1 stick lemongrass, roughly chopped

3 kaffir lime leaves

Sesame oil, for frying

¹/₃ cup (3¹/₂ oz/100 g) crunchy peanut butter

Zest of a lime, plus juice to taste

¹/₂ tsp black peppercorns, crushed

Sugar and salt to taste

SERVES 4 | *One serving shown*

PREP 15 mins, plus marinating

COOK 25–35 mins

A classic Indonesian dish, the name literally means "mix mix." Traditionally gado gado is served with crispy prawn crackers or cassava chips to give the dish added crunch.

Gado gado

FOR THE CHICKEN

- 1 red chili, finely chopped
- 2 cloves garlic, finely chopped
- 1 stalk lemongrass, finely chopped
- 1 tsp ground black pepper
- 1/4 tsp nutmeg, grated
- 1/2 tsp ground turmeric
- 1/2 tsp salt
- 3 tbsp sesame, peanut, or vegetable oil
- 1 lb 2 oz (500 g) chicken breast or thigh meat, sliced into strips
- 2 tbsp of vegetable oil, for frying

METHOD

1 Place all of the marinade ingredients in a large plastic food bag and add the chicken. Mix well, and leave in the refrigerator for a minimum of one hour or up to 12 hours—the longer it is left the stronger the flavor will be.

2 To make the peanut sauce: add the chilies, garlic, lemongrass, and lime leaves to a food processor and pulse to a coarse paste. Heat the sesame oil in a skillet and add the spicy paste; stir-fry for 5 minutes on a low heat. Add the peanut butter, lime zest and juice, black pepper, and 4 tablespoons of water. Stir well and cook on a low heat for 5 minutes, adding a splash more water if needed. Taste and add sugar, lime, salt, and pepper to taste.

3 To make the salad: cut the potatoes into quarters and place in a pan of cold water. Bring to the boil and simmer for 10–15 minutes, or until almost cooked. Add the beans to the boiling water for the final 2 minutes, and finally the cabbage for about 1 minute. Add the bean sprouts to the pan, and drain immediately. Leave the vegetables to stand for a couple of minutes and then cool under cold water and set aside.

4 Heat 2 tablespoons of oil in a wok or large skillet and add the marinated chicken. Stir-fry quickly until the chicken is cooked through and golden on the outside—about 5 to 10 minutes.

5 Arrange the cooked vegetables on a large serving plate and drizzle over the peanut sauce, add the stir-fried chicken on top and garnish with the hard-boiled eggs, cilantro, and chopped chili. Serve with the prawn crackers.

Tofu vegan gado gado

Replace the chicken with firm tofu and omit the eggs. To prepare the tofu: mix the marinade as for the chicken recipe and coat small blocks of tofu. Marinate for a minimum of one hour and a maximum of 12 hours. Heat the oil in a wok and stir-fry the tofu until it is golden and crispy all over—this should take 5–10 minutes.

SERVES 4

PREP 20 mins

COOK 5 mins

Packed full of zesty punch and with a lovely chili kick, this super low-fat noodle salad is one to wake up your tastebuds.

Gingered noodle salad with soy beans and shrimp

INGREDIENTS

Juice of 2 limes

2 tbsp fish sauce (nam pla)

2 long red chilies, deseeded and finely chopped

2 cloves garlic, crushed

A thumb-sized piece of fresh root ginger, finely grated

1 tsp sugar

Salt and freshly ground black pepper

12 oz (350 g) rice noodles

1 cup (10¹/₂ oz/300 g) soy beans, fresh or frozen

10¹/₂ oz (300 g) jumbo shrimp, cooked and peeled

6 scallions, finely sliced

TO GARNISH

2 tbsp roasted peanuts, roughly chopped

A handful of cilantro leaves

METHOD

1 In a large mixing bowl, whisk together the lime juice, fish sauce, chili, garlic, ginger, and sugar. Taste, adding a little salt and pepper if necessary.

2 Put the noodles in a heatproof bowl and completely cover in boiling water. Set aside to soften for 15 minutes, then drain, run under cold water to cool, then drain again. Toss well through the dressing.

3 Bring a pan of lightly salted water to the boil. Add the soy beans and cook until just tender, about 3–4 minutes. Drain the beans and add to the dressed noodles.

4 Mix through the shrimp and scallions. To serve, scatter over the peanuts and cilantro leaves.

Vegetarian gingered noodle salad

Omit the fish sauce, replacing it with 2 tbsp light soy sauce. Omit the shrimp and cook 10–12 baby sweet corn spears along with the soy beans. Drain and stir through the noodles, along with 1 finely sliced bell pepper.

Colorful and filling, these wraps are great for lunch on the go or a summer picnic. You can serve the salad, wraps, and tuna separately and let people construct their own wrap.

Southern bean salad and tuna wraps

F ★

SERVES 6 | *Two servings shown*

PREP 20 mins

INGREDIENTS

3 tbsp olive oil

1 tbsp white wine vinegar

1 tsp clear honey

1 clove garlic, crushed

Pinch dried chili flakes (optional)

Pinch dried thyme

2 x 14 oz (400 g) cans mixed beans (kidney, pinto, black-eyed, navy all work well)

1 x 7 oz (200 g) can sweet corn, drained

2 ripe avocados, sliced

2 bell peppers, thinly sliced

Small bunch of cilantro, chopped

Salt and freshly ground black pepper

6 large, soft tortillas

2 x 6 oz (170 g) cans tuna, drained

METHOD

1 In a medium bowl, whisk together the oil, vinegar, honey, garlic, chili, and thyme.

2 Add the beans, sweet corn, avocados, peppers, and cilantro and stir well. Season to taste with salt and pepper.

3 Spoon some of the mixture into the center of a flour tortilla. Top with tuna, tuck in the ends, securing the filling inside, and roll into a tight wrap. Wrap tightly in plastic wrap then cut in half. Repeat with the remaining tortillas.

SERVING SUGGESTION: Keep the wraps in parchment paper to keep them fresh.

Bean salad and griddled halloumi wraps

For an easy vegetarian alternative, replace the tuna with grilled halloumi. Replace the bell pepper with 4 large, ripe tomatoes, roughly chopped.

SERVES 4 | *One serving shown*

PREP 25 mins

COOK 1 hour 5 mins, plus cooling

This delicious Turkish meze dish is traditionally served cold as part of a buffet spread. The oil used to dress the salad adds much to the flavor, so use the best extra virgin olive oil you can find.

Cranberry bean pilaki

Pilaki is gluten-free if served plain

INGREDIENTS

1 large onion, finely chopped

3 tbsp olive oil

1 large eggplant, chopped into ½ in (1 cm) cubes

3 cloves garlic, crushed

Handful ripe cherry tomatoes, quartered

1 tbsp tomato puree

1 tsp sugar

Salt and freshly ground black pepper

1 x 14 oz (400 g) can cranberry beans, drained and rinsed

3 tbsp extra virgin olive oil

Juice of ½–1 lemon

Small bunch flat-leaf parsley, roughly chopped

METHOD

1 In a deep skillet, fry the onion in the oil over a medium heat for 10 minutes until soft and lightly caramelized.

2 Add the eggplant, reduce the heat a little and continue to fry for a further 15 minutes stirring frequently until the eggplant is slightly soft and colored in places.

3 Add the garlic, fry for a further minute before adding the tomatoes, tomato puree, sugar, and 1½ cups (375 ml) cold water. Season with a little salt and pepper, bring to the boil then reduce the heat to a steady simmer. Cook for 30 minutes until the sauce is thick and rich, adding a little more water if necessary. Add the beans and simmer gently for a further 10 minutes.

4 Allow to cool to room temperature, then dress with the extra virgin olive oil and lemon juice. Stir through the parsley, taste, and adjust seasoning.

SERVING SUGGESTION: Scoop up the pilaki with lightly toasted wholemeal pita bread, plus lemon wedges for squeezing and a parsley garnish.

Cranberry and carrot spiced pilaki

Substitute 3 thinly sliced carrots for the eggplant. Add spices to jazz it up a little—chili flakes or cumin, ground coriander, caraway, or fennel seeds would all work really well. Cranberry beans work well in pilaki because they are soft and yielding in texture. For a touch more bite use a firmer bean, such as cannellini or navy beans.

SNACKS AND DIPS

There is an endless array of dips to be made from beans, but the familiar hummus is a good place to start. These recipes are great for snacking or stand-up party food.

SERVES 4

PREP 10 mins

COOK 15–20 minutes

Hummus is the best known bean-based dip—this version is deep with flavor, with sweetness from the bell peppers.

Roasted garlic and red bell pepper hummus

Hummus is gluten-free if served plain

INGREDIENTS

2 red bell peppers

1 tbsp olive oil

3 cloves garlic, unpeeled

1 x 14 oz (400 g) can chickpeas, drained and rinsed

2 tbsp light tahini

2 tbsp olive oil

Juice of half a lemon

Salt and freshly ground black pepper

METHOD

1 Preheat the oven to 400°F (200°C/gas mark 6). Quarter the bell peppers and discard the seeds and white membranes. Lay in a roasting pan and drizzle over the olive oil, tuck in the garlic cloves and roast for 15–20 minutes, until soft and slightly colored at the edges. Remove from the oven, squeeze the garlic cloves from their skins, and add to a food processor. Tip in the red bell peppers, reserving a few strips for the garnish, and pulse to chop coarsely.

2 Add the chickpeas, tahini, olive oil, lemon juice, salt and pepper. Process until completely combined and smooth. If necessary, add a tablespoon or two of cold water to loosen to a dipping consistency. Transfer to a bowl and allow to rest for at least an hour before serving to allow the flavors to develop. Garnish with strips of roasted bell pepper. Store in the refrigerator for up to 5 days.

SERVING SUGGESTION: Cut flatbreads into strips, sprinkle with sea salt and spices, and bake to make chips you can dip into the hummus.

Caramelized onion hummus

Peel and quarter two red onions and roast them in place of the red bell peppers to make a caramelized onion version. The onions will take a little longer to roast—about 25–30 minutes. Be careful not to let them burn.

SERVES 4

PREP 5 mins

This tasty dip can be on the table in minutes and is a little like a high-fiber, low-fat version of taramosalata.

Cannellini bean and smoked salmon dip

INGREDIENTS

1 x 14 oz (400 g) can cannellini beans, drained and rinsed

4¹/₂ oz (125 g) smoked salmon

2 tbsp crème fraîche

Finely grated zest of a lemon

Lemon juice, to taste

1 small bunch of dill, finely chopped

Salt and freshly ground black pepper

METHOD

1 Add the the beans, smoked salmon, and crème fraîche to a food processor and pulse together until really smooth and creamy. Add the lemon zest, juice, dill and salt and pepper to taste, and process until well mixed. Garnish with dill, and serve immediately with toast or crackers, or refrigerate for up to 3 days.

SERVING SUGGESTION: This dip goes perfectly with lightly steamed asparagus spears or crudités.

Vegan eggplant and smoked paprika dip

Slice 1 large eggplant into ¹/₄ in (5 mm) strips. Brush lightly with olive oil and griddle in a hot pan until soft and lightly charred. Add to the food processor along with the beans and half a teaspoon of smoked paprika and process until smooth. Season to taste with lemon juice, salt, and pepper.

Moroccan inspired samosas

Make a Moroccan version by replacing the butter beans with chickpeas and using a Moroccan spice blend instead of curry powder. To make a Moroccan spice mix: dry-fry 1 tablespoon each of cumin seeds and coriander seeds, and grind in a pestle and mortar or electric spice grinder. Add 1 teaspoon each of ground turmeric, cinnamon, paprika, and ground ginger and $^1/_2$ teaspoon each ground allspice and chili powder and stir well. These are delicious made with $3^1/_2$ oz (100 g) crumbled feta added to the mixture. You can also add yogurt to the cilantro dip—either soy or dairy will work well.

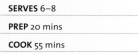

SERVES 6–8

PREP 20 mins

COOK 55 mins

Samosas are traditionally made with special samosa pastry, which needs to be deep fried. The samosas in this recipe are lower in fat because they are made with phyllo pastry, which can be baked.

Squash and butter bean samosas with cilantro chutney

F ♥ V V

Vegan if using oil to brush the phyllo

INGREDIENTS

1 lb 2 oz (500 g) butternut squash, peeled, deseeded, and chopped into ½ in (1 cm) cubes

3 scallions, finely chopped

2 cloves garlic, chopped

2 tbsp curry powder

2 red chilies, finely chopped

2 tbsp vegetable oil

1 x 14 oz (400 g) can butter beans, drained and rinsed

1 small bunch cilantro, chopped

½ cup (2 oz/60 g) frozen peas

Salt and freshly ground black pepper

Juice of half a lemon

9 oz (250 g) phyllo pastry

½ stick (2 oz/60 g) melted butter (or ¼ cup vegetable oil if vegan)

FOR THE CHUTNEY

1 small bunch cilantro

1 clove garlic, chopped

3 green chilies (or less, for a milder chutney)

1 tbsp brown sugar, or to taste

1 tsp salt, or to taste

Juice of half a lemon, or to taste

METHOD

1 Preheat the oven to 400°F (200°C/gas mark 6). Place the squash, scallions, garlic, curry powder and chili in a baking pan. Pour over the 2 tablespoons of vegetable oil, and mix well. Place in the center of the oven and roast for 30 minutes, turning once. Remove from the oven, add the butter beans and stir well, return to the oven for a further 10 minutes.

2 Remove the vegetables from the oven and allow to cool. Gently mash the vegetables with a potato masher. Add the chopped cilantro and frozen peas (no need to defrost them), salt, pepper, and lemon juice to taste.

3 Place the phyllo pastry on a dry surface and slice lengthwise through the pastry so that you have strips approximately 4 in (10 cm) wide. Take one strip, brush with the melted butter or oil, and layer another strip on top. Place a tablespoon of filling at one end of the phyllo strip and fold over the bottom left corner of the pastry to make a triangle shape. Continue to fold the filling up along the length of the pastry in this manner, until you reach the end. Brush the outside of the samosa with butter or oil and place on a cookie sheet. Repeat until you have used up all of the pastry and filling. Bake the samosas for 10–15 minutes or until golden and crispy—turn halfway through cooking.

4 To prepare the chutney: place the cilantro, garlic, and chillies in a food processor or in a jug with a stick blender and puree until smooth. Taste and add sugar, salt, and lemon juice to your taste. Serve the samosas warm, with the cilantro chutney on the side.

SERVES 4 | *Two servings shown*

PREP 15 mins

COOK 40–55 mins

Quesadillas are just about the perfect comfort food— crispy, gooey, and loved by everyone. At a party, these will disappear in minutes.

Black-eyed pea quesadillas

V

FOR THE BEANS

2 tbsp olive oil

1 onion, chopped

2 garlic cloves, minced

1 tsp cumin seeds

1 tsp paprika

Pinch dried chili flakes (optional)

1 x 14 oz (400 g) can black-eyed peas, drained and rinsed

1 cup (250 ml) vegetable stock

Salt and freshly ground black pepper

FOR THE QUESADILLAS

6 large soft flour tortillas

1 x 7 oz (200 g) can sweet corn, drained

Handful cherry tomatoes, quartered

2 cups (9 oz/250 g) mature Cheddar cheese, grated

1 small bunch cilantro, chopped

3 tbsp crème fraîche or soured cream

A little vegetable oil for shallow frying

METHOD

1 To make the beans: heat the oil in a skillet and fry the onion over a medium heat for 10–15 minutes until softened and starting to caramelize. Add the garlic, cumin, paprika, and chili (if using) and stir-fry for a further minute.

2 Tip in the beans and the stock and bring up to the boil. Simmer for 10–15 minutes until the beans have partially broken down and you are left with a thick, rich mixture. Season to taste with salt and pepper.

3 Divide this mixture evenly between 3 of the flour tortillas, spreading out all over but leaving a 1/2 in (1 cm) margin around the edge, and scatter the sweet corn, tomatoes, cheese, and cilantro over the top. Spread the remaining tortillas with a little crème fraîche, and use to top the quesadillas, pressing spread-side down firmly to make 3 sandwiches.

4 Heat a little oil in a skillet large enough to hold one quesadilla. When hot, carefully lower in a quesadilla and fry over a medium heat for 4–5 minutes until crisp. Using a fish slice, carefully turn over and fry for a further 2–3 minutes on the other side. Transfer to a plate and keep warm while you repeat with the other quesadillas. Serve warm, cut into wedges.

SERVING SUGGESTION: Give each guest their own stack of quesadilla wedges on a square of parchment paper.

Refried bean quesadilla with chicken

Try using red kidney beans in place of black-eyed peas, or for a super-speedy snack you could use ready-made refried beans. You can also add a little shredded chicken when you scatter over the sweet corn and tomatoes, and serve with the carrot relish on page 47.

SERVES	4
PREP	5 mins
COOK	30–40 mins

Once you have made these spicy chickpeas you'll be hooked—they are incredibly tasty and make the perfect snack—a great alternative to potato chips.

Spicy roasted chickpea "chips"

INGREDIENTS

2 x 14 oz (400 g) cans chickpeas, drained and rinsed

2 tsp olive oil

2 tsp ground cumin seeds

2 tsp ground coriander

1 tsp dried chili flakes

Sea salt flakes, to taste

METHOD

1 Preheat the oven to 425°F (220°C/gas mark 7). Spread the chickpeas out on paper towels and pat dry.

2 Transfer to a baking pan, drizzle over the oil, and sprinkle over the spices and salt, tossing well to coat. Roast for 30–35 minutes until crisp all the way through. If they are still soft, roast for a few more minutes.

New favorite flavors

The spices can be easily varied to change the style of this bar snack—try tossing in curry powder for a "Bombay mix," or smoked paprika and garlic powder for a Spanish twist.

Get ahead of the party

The unfried croquetas will
rest quite happily in the
refrigerator for up to 24
hours, making it a good
task to do ahead of time.

SERVES 6–8

PREP 20 mins, plus chilling

COOK 35–45 mins, plus frying time

These crisp, savory croquetas are great for a party, and taste delicious dipped in a little green pesto or tomato relish.

Butter bean, eggplant, and Parmesan croquetas

When vegetarian cheese used

INGREDIENTS

1 large eggplant (about 1 lb 2 oz/500 g)

2 tbsp olive oil

1 onion, very finely chopped

2 cloves garlic, minced

1 tbsp finely chopped fresh rosemary

2 x 14 oz (400 g) cans butter beans, drained and rinsed

1 cup (3¹/₂ oz/100 g) Parmesan, grated

¹/₂ cup (2 oz/60 g) ground almonds

3 large eggs, beaten

Salt and freshly ground black pepper

2 cups (7 oz/200 g) fine, dried breadcrumbs

Vegetable oil, for deep frying

METHOD

1 Preheat the oven to 350°F (180°C/gas mark 4). Prick the eggplant all over with a fork, place in a baking pan, and roast whole for about 35–45 minutes until soft to the touch. Allow to cool a little before peeling and roughly chopping the flesh.

2 While the eggplant is cooking, warm the olive oil in a small skillet over a low heat. Gently sweat the onion with the garlic and rosemary until it is soft and translucent, about 15 minutes.

3 Tip the softened onion mixture into a food processor, along with the chopped eggplant flesh, the butter beans, Parmesan, ground almonds, and one of the beaten eggs. Process until a smooth paste is formed. Season generously with salt and freshly ground black pepper. Chill in the refrigerator for an hour or so for the flavors to mingle and the mixture to firm up a little.

4 When you are ready to begin shaping the croquetas, set yourself up a production line with the 2 beaten eggs in a small, shallow bowl, and the breadcrumbs on a large plate. Take a tablespoon of the chilled mixture and, using slightly wet hands, press into a croqueta shape. Drop gently into the egg then lift out and roll in the breadcrumbs until coated all over. Transfer to a clean plate. Repeat with the remaining mixture then chill again for at least 30 minutes.

5 To cook, heat the oil in a deep-fat fryer to 350°F (180°C) and fry in batches for about 4–5 minutes until crisp and golden. Drain on paper towels and serve immediately.

SERVING SUGGESTION: Serve with green tarragon pesto, see page 40.

SERVES 4

PREP 15 mins

A surprisingly light and refreshing dip with an attention-grabbing color, this dip is sure to be the talk of your get-together.

Herbed butter bean, beet, and walnut puree

INGREDIENTS

- ¹/₂ cup (1³/₄ oz/50 g) walnut halves
- 1³/₄ cups (9 oz/250 g) cooked beets
- 1 x 14 oz (400 g) can butter beans, drained and rinsed
- 1 clove garlic, crushed
- 2 tbsp red wine vinegar
- 2 tbsp extra virgin olive oil
- A generous handful of leafy mixed herbs, roughly chopped (cilantro, dill, and parsley work well)
- Salt and freshly ground black pepper

METHOD

1 Add the walnuts to a food processor and process until they are ground to fine crumbs. Add the beets, butter beans, and garlic and process until quite smooth.

2 With the motor running, trickle in the red wine vinegar and olive oil. Add just enough cold water to bring everything together as a smooth paste—you may not need any. Finally add the herbs and process until just combined. Set aside for 30 minutes at room temperature to allow the flavors to develop.

SERVING SUGGESTION: Spoon the dip into red Belgian endive leaves to serve as hors d'oeuvres, or serve red Belgian endive leaves on the side of a bowl of the dip.

Spiced carrot, butter bean, and almond dip

Cook 10¹/₂ oz (300 g) carrots until soft, drain, and add to the food processor along with the butter beans and garlic. Add ¹/₄ cup (2 oz/60 g) ground almonds, 1 teaspoon each of ground cumin, ground coriander, and smoked paprika and continue as above.

Lamb and cilantro phyllo rolls

Heat a splash of oil in a skillet and add 7 oz (200 g) ground lamb. Sprinkle in 2 teaspoons each of lightly crushed cumin and coriander seeds, plus dried chili to taste. Fry over a high heat until crisp. Transfer to a plate and set aside. Use the same pan to fry the onions and continue as for the recipe above, omitting the caraway seeds and smoked paprika. Do not add the feta cheese, but fold the crisp meat through the onion and chickpea mix, adding a generous handful of roughly chopped cilantro as you do so. Allow the filling to cool before stuffing and rolling as right.

SERVES 4 | *Two servings shown*

PREP 15 mins

COOK 30 mins

These spring-roll shaped snacks are the perfect finger food. The smoked paprika flavoring will make them a favorite for "meatless Mondays."

Feta and chickpea phyllo rolls

INGREDIENTS

2 onions, chopped

2 tbsp olive oil

1 tsp dried chili flakes

1 tsp smoked paprika

1 tsp caraway seeds

2 cloves garlic, minced

1 x 14 oz (400 g) can chickpeas, drained and rinsed

Salt and freshly ground black pepper

1³/₄ cups (7 oz/200 g) feta cheese, crumbled

9¹/₂ oz (270 g) phyllo pastry

³/₄ stick (75 g) butter, melted

METHOD

1 In a large, deep skillet, sweat the onions in the olive oil for 10 minutes until softening. Add the chili, paprika, and caraway and fry gently for a further 10 minutes until the onion is very soft and lightly caramelized. Add the garlic and fry for just another minute or so. Stir through the chickpeas, and season well with salt and freshly ground black pepper. Remove from the heat and leave to cool.

2 Once the filling is cool, gently stir through the feta, trying not to break it up too much.

3 Unroll the sheets of phyllo and cut each in half. Cover loosely with damp paper towels to stop the sheets drying and cracking. Take one sheet, brush with a little melted butter, then fold in half to give you a double-thickness rectangle. Spoon a little of the filling along a shorter side, shaping it into a rough sausage, and taking care to leave a ¹/₄ in (5 mm) border along the edges. Tightly roll into a tube, tucking and sealing the ends in as you go. Brush a little more butter along the seal to stick together. Lightly brush butter all over the sealed roll, and lay on a baking pan. Repeat until you have finished all the phyllo. At this point, the rolls can be chilled in the refrigerator for up to 12 hours, or frozen flat on a tray so they don't start to stick together. Defrost in the refrigerator overnight before cooking.

4 When you are ready to bake, heat the oven to 400°F (200°C/gas mark 6). Cook for 12–15 minutes, turning once, until crisp and deeply golden. Allow to cool a little before eating as the cheese will be very hot.

SERVES 4	
PREP 5 mins	
COOK 5 mins	

This super-simple, healthy, and tasty dip takes minutes to make and is great with crisp pita bread or a selection of crudités.

Broad bean, mint, and ricotta dip

INGREDIENTS

1²/₃ cups (9 oz/250 g) baby broad beans (shelled weight), fresh or frozen

¹/₄ cup (3¹/₂ oz/100 g) ricotta cheese

1 small bunch of mint leaves, chopped

1 clove garlic, minced

Pinch dried chili flakes (optional)

Squeeze of lemon juice, to taste

Salt and freshly ground black pepper

METHOD

1 Plunge the broad beans into a saucepan of boiling water and cook until just tender, about 5 minutes. Drain well, add to a food processor, and process until smooth.

2 Add the ricotta, mint, garlic, and chili flakes, if using, and process again.

3 Season to taste with a squeeze of lemon juice and salt and pepper. Serve warm or at room temperature.

SERVING SUGGESTION: Serve this dip with bread sticks or stacks of sliced ciabatta bread.

Pea, chive, and blue cheese dip

Use the same weight of peas, fresh or frozen, in place of the broad beans. Substitute the mint for a small bunch of chopped chives and replace the ricotta cheese with a creamy, soft blue cheese.

Freeze easy

Use frozen baby broad
beans when fresh
aren't in season, they
are just as nutritious
and very convenient.

Spice variations

For a Middle Eastern flavor, cook the onion with a mix of ground cumin, crushed coriander seeds, and ground coriander.

For a Spanish-inspired egg, omit all of the spices; instead fry 1 teaspoon of smoked paprika and 3 oz (75 g) finely chopped chorizo sausage with the onion.

For a Thai-inspired version, substitute finely chopped Kaffir lime leaves and a lemongrass stalk for all of the spices. Spread the inside of the flattened mix with a little sweet chili sauce in place of the mango chutney before rolling up.

SERVES 4 | *One serving shown*

PREP 15 mins

COOK 30 mins

An adaptable snack that you can give a global flavor if you vary the spices you add when you are cooking the onion—the main recipe uses a mix of Indian spices.

Spiced bean savory eggs with mango chutney

V

INGREDIENTS

6 medium eggs

2 tbsp olive oil

1 small onion, finely chopped

2 cloves garlic, minced

2 tsp ground cumin

2 tsp ground coriander

1 tsp cayenne pepper

1 tsp ground turmeric

1 tsp ground ginger

1 x 14 oz (400 g) can chickpeas, drained and rinsed

Salt and freshly ground black pepper

4 heaped tsp mango chutney

1¼ cups (4 oz/120 g) fresh breadcrumbs

Vegetable oil, for deep frying

METHOD

1 Take four of the eggs and place in a small saucepan. Cover with cold water and bring to the boil, reduce the heat to a simmer, and cook for 5 minutes. Remove from the heat, run under cold water until cool enough to handle, peel, and set aside. Crack the other two eggs into a bowl and lightly beat. Set aside.

2 Heat the oil in a small skillet and gently sweat the onion until beginning to soften, about 10 minutes. Add the garlic and the spices and fry gently for another couple of minutes. Tip into a food processor along with the chickpeas and a couple of tablespoons of water. Season well with salt and pepper, and process until smooth. Transfer to a bowl and chill in the refrigerator for at least an hour to firm up.

3 Divide the chickpea mix into four balls, flattening each into a disc. Spoon a heaped teaspoon of mango chutney into the center of each disc and spread out almost to the edges. Place an egg in the center and carefully draw up the sides to completely enclose the egg within the chickpea mix. Repeat with the other three balls of chickpea mix.

4 Dip each savory-egg ball into the beaten egg, then roll in the breadcrumbs until coated. Once all are coated, repeat the egg dipping and breadcrumb rolling to give them a second coat.

5 Heat the vegetable oil in a deep-fat fryer to 350°F (180°C) and cook the coated eggs for 5–6 minutes until crisp and golden. Serve warm or cold.

SERVING SUGGESTION: Serve with a light green side salad.

SWEET BEANS

Can a chocolate brownie ever be good for you? This chapter has some
delicious treats to try at any time of day, plus some sweet ways to start the day,
full of the goodness of beans.

Dorayaki pancakes

These Japanese sweet snacks are made by sandwiching adzuki bean paste (called "Anko" in Japanese) between two sweet pancakes. Use the filling paste in the Mooncake recipe (with or without the cashew nuts). Make the pancakes by whisking together 1³/₄ cups (7 oz/200 g) all-purpose flour, 2 tsp baking powder, 2 eggs and 2 tsp sugar—make sure there are no lumps. Add 1¹/₄ cups (300 ml) of milk gradually so that you have a smooth, thick batter with the consistency of heavy cream. Heat a skillet and melt a little butter or oil. Ladle 1 tbsp of pancake mixture into the pan and cook on both sides until golden. Place a cooked pancake on a plate, lay a spoonful of the adzuki paste on top, sandwich another pancake on top and press all around the edges to seal. Repeat until you have used all of the pancake batter and adzuki paste.

MAKES 10

PREP 10 mins, plus 1 hour resting

COOK 25 mins

Mooncakes are made in parts of China to celebrate the mid-Autumn festival. They are traditionally made in an ornately patterned mold—without the mold they make pebble-shaped cookies.

Mooncake cookies

Vegan if brushed with oil instead of egg

FOR THE DOUGH

$^1/_4$ cup (2$^1/_2$ oz/70 g) corn syrup

2 tbsp vegetable oil

1 tbsp hot water

1 cup (3$^1/_2$ oz/100 g) all-purpose flour

FOR THE FILLING

$^1/_4$ cup (1 oz/30 g) raw cashew nuts

1 x 14 oz (400 g) can adzuki beans, drained and rinsed

3 tbsp sugar (or more to taste, fine ground sugars such as superfine work best)

1 beaten egg to glaze (or 2 tbsp vegetable oil if vegan)

Powdered sugar for dusting

METHOD

1 To prepare the dough: in a small bowl mix together the corn syrup, oil, and hot water. Gradually add the flour a little at a time to form a soft dough, adding a little more flour if it is very sticky. Knead the dough for 2 minutes and then roll into a ball and wrap tightly in plastic wrap. Place in the refrigerator for 1 hour to rest.

2 Preheat the oven to 400°F (200°C/gas mark 6). To prepare the filling: grind the cashews in a food processor and set aside. Place the drained beans and sugar in the food processor and puree until smooth. Combine the beans and cashews and taste—add a little more sugar if needed. Divide the mixture into 10 balls.

3 Dust a worktop with powdered sugar. Roll a ball of dough out into a circle 2$^1/_2$–3 in (6–7 cm) in diameter. Pick up the dough carefully and place a spoonful of the filling in the center. Carefully gather the edges of the dough together to form a ball. Turn the ball over so that the untidy edges are underneath, and gently pat around the edges until it is a perfect round shape with a flattened top.

4 Place the moon cakes on a baking pan lined with parchment paper and bake for 10 minutes. Remove from the oven and cool for 10 minutes and then brush with the beaten egg (or oil if vegan) and return to the oven for a further 15 minutes or until golden all over. Serve warm or cold with Chinese tea.

MAKES 12

PREP 15 mins

COOK 20 mins

These rich and intensely chocolaty brownies have a secret fiber-boost from the addition of black beans— a great way to make them a healthier treat.

Chocolate and orange brownies   F ★ V

INGREDIENTS

1 x 14 oz (400 g) can black beans, drained and rinsed

1¹/₂ cups (7 oz/200 g) dark chocolate squares (70 percent cocoa solids), melted

3 large eggs

4 tbsp sunflower or vegetable oil

²/₃ cup (4¹/₂ oz/125 g) sugar (fine ground sugars such as superfine work best)

²/₃ cup (2¹/₂ oz/75 g) all-purpose flour

3 tbsp cocoa powder

2 tsp vanilla extract

Zest of 2 large oranges

2 tsp baking powder

¹/₂ tsp baking soda

2–3 tbsp milk

METHOD

1 Preheat the oven to 350°F (180°C/gas mark 4). Tip the beans into a food processor and process until ground to a crumbly paste. Add the melted chocolate, eggs, and oil and process until smooth. Then add the sugar, flour, cocoa powder, vanilla, orange zest, baking powder, and baking soda and process until blended. Finally, add enough milk to loosen the mixture to a soft dropping consistency.

2 Grease and line a 10 in (25 cm) square baking pan with parchment paper and pour in the brownie mixture, leveling with a table knife.

3 Bake for about 20 minutes until the top is crisp and the brownie is starting to come away from the edges of the pan. Allow to cool completely in the the pan before cutting into 12 squares.

SERVING SUGGESTION: Dust with powdered sugar or a little extra grated orange zest to garnish.

Cranberry brownies and zesty frosting

For a seasonal variation, exchange the orange zest for ¹/₂ cup (4¹/₂ oz/125 g) dried cranberries. Add frosting to either recipe for a zesty lift: blend ¹/₂ cup (4¹/₂ oz/125 g) cream cheese and ¹/₂ stick (1³/₄ oz/50 g) butter, softened with 4³/₄ cups (1 lb/450 g) powdered sugar and 2 tablespoons lemon juice.

| MAKES 2–3 smoothies |
| PREP 5 mins |

Pink and perfect, this is a great on-the-go breakfast for health conscious foodies and sweet-toothed smoothie lovers alike. The beans do not come across in the flavor, but they do add a lovely creamy texture.

Berry bean breakfast smoothie

Vegan if no yogurt added

INGREDIENTS

1 banana

Handful mixed berries (strawberries, blueberries, raspberries)

1/2 cup (2 oz/60 g) canned white beans (such as cannellini or butter beans), drained and rinsed

1/2 cup (125 ml) apple juice

1 tbsp Greek yogurt (optional)

1/4 tsp vanilla extract (optional)

METHOD

1 The method is very simple: just add everything to a liquidizer and process until completely smooth.

SERVING SUGGESTION: Garnish with a fresh raspberry.

Sweet, zingy breakfast smoothie

Replace the berries with fresh pineapple, and the vanilla with 1 teaspoon of freshly grated fresh root ginger.

SERVES 8

PREP 15 mins, plus chilling

COOK 50 mins

As rich and decadent as all good cheesecakes should be, this one is a little healthier—with added fiber and nutrients, thanks to the beans.

Cappuccino navy bean cheesecake

V

FOR THE CRUST

1³/₄ cups (6¹/₄ oz/175 g) graham crackers

¹/₄ cup (2 oz/50 g) sugar

¹/₂ stick (2 oz/50 g) butter, melted, plus extra for greasing

FOR THE FILLING

1 x 14 oz (400 g) cans navy beans, drained and rinsed

1¹/₄ cups (10¹/₂ oz/300 g) cream cheese

³/₄ cup (7 oz/200 g) crème fraîche

3 large eggs

1 cup (8 oz/200 g) sugar (fine ground sugars such as superfine work best)

1 tsp vanilla extract

1 tbsp espresso-strength coffee

FOR THE TOPPING

²/₃ cup (5¹/₂ oz/150 g) crème fraîche

1 tbsp sugar (fine ground sugars such as superfine work best)

1 tsp vanilla extract

Grated dark chocolate to decorate

METHOD

1 Preheat the oven to 325°F (160°C/gas mark 3). Line the base of a 10 in (25 cm) round springform pan with parchment paper and butter the sides. Fit a double layer sheet of foil under the baking pan and bring it up around the sides so that it fits tightly—this will protect the cheesecake when you cook it in the water bath.

2 To make the crust: add the crackers to a food processor and process to fine crumbs. Pour in the sugar and butter, and blend until combined. Spread evenly into the prepared pan, firming with the back of a spoon. Place in the refrigerator while you make the topping.

3 For the filling: add the beans to the cleaned food processor bowl and process until finely ground. Add the cream cheese, crème fraîche, eggs, sugar, vanilla, and coffee and process until completely smooth and creamy. Pour over the crumb base and lower the pan, foil jacket and all, into a large, deep-sided roasting pan. Pour in enough hot water to come halfway up the sides, carefully transfer to the oven and bake for 50 minutes.

4 While the cheesecake bakes, make the topping: whisk the crème fraîche, sugar, and vanilla in a small bowl.

5 Once the cheesecake has baked, remove from the oven and carefully pour the topping over, spreading with a table knife. Allow to cool in the pan. When cool, transfer to the refrigerator and chill for at least 4 hours. Remove from the pan and decorate with grated chocolate before serving.

Lemon cheesecake with raspberries and white chocolate

Add the finely grated zest of a lemon and a tablespoon of lemon juice to the cheesecake mix in place of the coffee. Omit the crème fraîche topping and cook for a total of 50 minutes. Once the cheesecake has cooled completely, decorate the top with 8 oz (225 g) fresh raspberries. Melt ½ cup (3 oz/80 g) white chocolate chips and use a teaspoon to drizzle over the raspberries. Allow to set before slicing and serving.

MAKES 12

PREP 15 mins

COOK 20–25 mins

Packed with plenty of nutritious beans, fruit, and nuts, these muffins make a healthy breakfast treat.

Spiced pinto bean, oat, and apple muffins

F ⬤ ★ V

INGREDIENTS

1 x 14 oz (400 g) can pinto beans, drained and rinsed

3 large eggs

$^1/_2$ stick + 3 tbsp (3$^1/_2$ oz/100 g) butter, melted and cooled

$^1/_2$ cup (3$^1/_2$ oz/100 g) dark brown sugar

3 small apples (about $^3/_4$ lb/350 g), peeled, cored, and grated

2$^2/_3$ cups (9 oz/250 g) ground almonds

2 tsp ground mixed spice

2 tsp baking powder

$^1/_2$ cup (3$^1/_2$ oz/100 g) raisins

$^1/_3$ cup (2 oz/60 g) oats, plus a few extra for sprinkling on top

Clear honey to drizzle

METHOD

1 Preheat the oven to 350°F (180°C/gas mark 4). Line a 12-hole muffin pan with paper cases.

2 Add the beans to a food processor and process finely. Add the eggs, butter, and sugar and blend together until smooth and creamy.

3 Transfer to a mixing bowl and add the grated apple, almonds, spices, and baking powder and beat until well combined.

4 Fold through the raisins and oats, and spoon the mixture into the paper cases. Sprinkle a few extra oats on top of each muffin and bake in the oven for 20–25 minutes until springy to the touch. Before serving, drizzle a little honey on top of the muffins.

Spiced pinto bean, carrot, and date muffins

Simply substitute the apple for the same amount of grated carrot, and the raisins for the same weight of chopped dates.

| SERVES 4–6 |
| COOK 45 mins, plus chilling and churning |

PREP 10 mins

This rich and creamy ice cream is sure to be a hit—no one will ever guess it contains beans.

Cinnamon, orange, and white bean ice cream

INGREDIENTS

1 x 14 oz (400 g) can of cannellini beans, drained and rinsed

1 scant cup (200 ml) whole milk

Zest of 2 large oranges

1 cinnamon stick

1 cup (250 ml) heavy cream

²/₃ cup (4¹/₂ oz/125 g) superfine sugar

3 egg yolks

METHOD

1 Put the beans in a medium saucepan with a tight-fitting lid. Pour over the milk and add the orange zest and cinnamon stick. Bring to the boil, reduce the heat to a very gentle simmer and cover tightly. Cook for 30 minutes, or until the beans are very soft. Remove from the heat, and discard the cinnamon stick. Add the bean mix to a food processor or blender, processing until smooth.

2 Add the cream, sugar, and the egg yolks to the blender and blitz again. Pour back into the cleaned saucepan and set over a very low heat, stirring frequently, for about 10 minutes, until the custard thickens. Remove from the heat.

3 Pour the mixture into a bowl, and then gently press a layer of plastic wrap over the surface to prevent a skin forming. Place in the refrigerator to chill completely.

4 Once cold, churn in an ice cream machine until frozen. This has a slightly harder scooping texture than traditional ice cream and benefits from allowing to thaw at room temperature for half an hour before serving.

SERVING SUGGESTION: Sprinkle with ground cinnamon and crushed cookies.

Chocolate-chip bean ice cream

Omit the orange zest and cinnamon stick. Use 2 generous teaspoons of vanilla extract in their place, then proceed as in the recipe. Just before churning the chilled custard, fold through 1 cup (6 oz/170 g) semisweet chocolate chips or the same amount of good quality chocolate, roughly chopped.

SERVES 2 | *One serving shown*

PREP 10 mins, plus overnight soaking

COOK 1 hour

Red bean soup is a popular dessert in Japan and China. The soup is rich and warming—real comfort food. This recipe includes coconut milk for extra flavor.

Sweet red bean soup

INGREDIENTS

¹/₂ cup (5¹/₂ oz/150 g) dried adzuki beans, soaked overnight

Zest and juice of 1 tangerine

4 cups (1 l) water

³/₄ cup (165 ml) coconut milk

4 tbsp light brown sugar

Pinch of salt

METHOD

1 Drain the soaked beans and place in a large saucepan with the tangerine zest and 2 cups (500 ml) of the water. Bring to the boil and simmer for about an hour, until the beans are really soft. As the beans are cooking, gradually add the rest of the water—adding it a little at a time means that the beans become soft and develop a thick red cooking liquid that adds to the texture and color of the soup.

2 When the beans are fully soft, remove half of them and puree until smooth with a stick blender (or in a food processor). Return the pureed beans to the pan, and add a pinch of salt and the tangerine juice, and simmer for 5 minutes.

3 Add the coconut milk to the soup and taste, before adding as much or as little sugar as you like. Serve the soup hot or just-warm in small bowls.

SERVING SUGGESTION: Garnish with a little tangerine zest and a drizzle of coconut milk or cream. If you prefer a smoother texture, puree all the finished soup and serve chilled.

Red bean Popsicles

Make the soup as described above and spoon into Popsicle molds. Freeze and enjoy! Alternatively, you can churn the mixture in an ice cream maker to make delicious vegan ice cream.

MAKES 12

PREP 15 mins

COOK 20 mins

Blondies are a delicious white chocolate variation of brownies. White chocolate is so rich you don't need to add any extra fat and the blondies have extra fiber thanks to the cannellini beans.

Cannellini bean, white chocolate, and hazelnut blondies

★ V

INGREDIENTS

1 x 14 oz (400 g) can cannellini beans, drained and rinsed

1 1/2 cups (7 oz/200 g) white chocolate squares, melted

3 large eggs

2/3 cup (4 1/2 oz/125 g) sugar (fine ground sugars such as superfine work best)

2/3 cup (2 1/2 oz/75 g) all-purpose flour

2 tsp vanilla extract

2 tsp baking powder

1/2 tsp baking soda

3/4 cup (3 1/2 oz/100 g) hazelnuts, roughly chopped

1/2 cup (3 1/2 oz/100 g) white chocolate chips

METHOD

1 Preheat the oven to 350°F (180°C/gas mark 4). Tip the beans into a food processor and whizz until ground to a crumbly paste. Add the melted white chocolate and eggs, and process until smooth. Then add the sugar, flour, vanilla, baking powder, and baking soda and blend together.

2 Grease and line a 10 in (25 cm) square baking pan with parchment paper and pour in the blondie mixture, leveling with a table knife. Sprinkle the hazelnuts and white chocolate chips evenly over the surface.

3 Bake for about 20 minutes until the top is crisp and the blondie is starting to come away from the edges of the pan. Allow to cool completely in the the pan, before cutting into 12 squares.

White chocolate, raspberry, and lemon blondies

Fold 1 cup (4 1/2 oz/125 g) fresh raspberries and the finely grated zest of a lemon through the blondie mixture before pouring into the pan and leveling. Sprinkle over the white chocolate chips but omit the hazelnuts.

SERVES 8 | *Two servings shown*

PREP 20 mins, plus 6 hours soaking

COOK 30 mins

Served with a generous dollop of crème fraîche, a slice of this rich cake makes a comforting dessert. And it's gluten-free to boot.

Amaretto chocolate soufflé cake   F ⚫ ★ V

INGREDIENTS

$^1/_2$ cup (125 ml) amaretto

2 cups (10$^1/_2$ oz/300 g) prunes

1$^1/_2$ cups (7 oz/200 g) dark chocolate squares (70 percent cocoa solids)

1 stick + 1 tbsp (4$^1/_2$ oz/125 g) butter, cubed

1 x 14 oz (400 g) can white beans (such as cannellini or butter beans), drained and rinsed

$^3/_4$ cup (5$^1/_4$ oz/150 g) sugar (fine ground sugars such as superfine work best)

4 large eggs, separated

METHOD

1 Pour the amaretto over the prunes and cover tightly with plastic wrap. Warm in the microwave for 1 minute, then set aside to soak for at least 6 hours, and ideally overnight. Alternatively, warm the amaretto in a small saucepan, and pour over the prunes before soaking.

2 When you are ready to bake the cake, preheat the oven to 350°F (180°C/ gas mark 4), and grease and line a 9 in (23 cm) round springform baking pan. Place the chocolate squares and butter in a small heatproof bowl. Set over a pan of gently simmering water and allow to melt, stirring occasionally.

3 In a food processor, puree the beans until they are finely crumbled, then add the sugar and egg yolks and blend together until smooth. Add the melted chocolate and butter, and half the prunes along with any residual soaking liquor and blend until smooth and well combined.

4 Whisk the eggs whites until stiff. Add a couple of spoons of the chocolate mixture to the beaten egg white, mixing together thoroughly—this loosens the mixture a little and makes folding easier. Then use a metal spoon to gently fold the rest of the chocolate mixture in, along with the remaining prunes, taking care not to overmix or you will lose air from the egg whites. Transfer to the prepared baking pan, and bake for 30 minutes. Remove from the oven, and allow to cool in the pan.

Apricot, orange, and hazelnut soufflé cake

For an alcohol-free, citrus-spiked cake, substitute the prunes for an equal weight of dried apricots. Add to a small pan and pour over $^1/_2$ cup (125 ml) fresh orange juice and 2 wide strips of orange peel. Bring to the boil, reduce the heat to a very gentle simmer and cook, covered, for 5 minutes. Remove from the heat and allow to soak for 6 hours or overnight. Make the cake as above, folding in $^3/_4$ cup (3$^1/_2$ oz/100 g) roughly chopped hazelnuts with the softened apricots just before spooning into the pan.

INDEX OF RECIPES BY BEAN

GENERAL INDEX

Acknowledgments

I've enjoyed writing this book so much, not least because of all the help from my "cooking buddy" Jo Ingleby—what fun we had in the kitchen, what fun we had at the dining table. Thanks Jo for all you hard work in getting these recipes tested to perfection.

I'm very grateful to Sorrel Wood for trusting me with this project—thanks for setting me the challenge to make beans interesting and accessible to all. Huge thanks also to Philippa Davis for her hard work in getting everything and everyone organized. Simon Pask gets a special mention for bringing my recipes alive with his lovely photographs—thanks Simon! Thanks to go to Lucy Parissi and Nikki Ingram for their design and production.

Thanks to my agent, Kate Hordern, for her support, encouragement, and general enthusiasm for my recipes and my writing. Cheers Kate!

And last on my list are those very much first in my mind—thanks and love to Rob, Izaac, and Eve. As always.